The
Basic Skills
Agency

fresh start
in the workplace

Getting the basics right in
Construction
(Plant and Accessing)

Plant Maintenance

– Specialised Plant and Machinery Operations
– Accessing Operations and Rigging

Mapping the Adult Literacy and Numeracy Standards
to the occupational standards of the
Construction Industry Training Board

CITB

Published July 2001

ISBN 1 85990 167 0

Design: Studio 21

Contents

1. Introduction

By basic skills we mean:

> **" the ability to read, write and speak in English and to use mathematics at a level necessary to function and progress at work and in society in general. "**

The Government's National Strategy for basic skills has identified clear targets for improving levels of literacy and numeracy amongst the general population. Research has shown that almost one in four adults has difficulties with literacy and even greater numbers need help with numeracy.

> **" People at work need good basic skills not just because of the needs of a particular job. Such abilities are essential to perform a wide range of activities safely and effectively within the workplace. "**
> *Improving literacy and numeracy – A fresh start* (DfEE, 1999)

Many of the adults with poor literacy and numeracy skills are in the workplace or are undergoing occupational training. The national strategy for improving adult literacy and numeracy skills makes clear the important contribution that can be made by National Training Organisations.

> **" NTOs have a key role, and literacy and numeracy skills should be a key feature of their workforce development plans. "**
> *Skills for Life* (DfEE, 2001)

The Basic Skills Agency has been working closely with NTOs to map their occupational standards to the *National Standards for Adult Literacy and Adult Numeracy*. These maps are intended for use in training and development for all staff within the sector.

We have worked closely with each National Training Organisation to ensure that the basic skills standards in these maps reflect the range of skills and knowledge required by workers to perform the occupational tasks.

The occupational standards, have been mapped to the *National Standards for Adult Literacy and Adult Numeracy* at the appropriate level; either Entry 3, Level 1 or Level 2. Careful account has been taken of the basic skills demands of jobs and the National Training Organisation has contributed to this process by providing examples of work instructions, health and safety guidelines and other materials in use in the workplace and in training. The National Training Organisation has also been fully involved in the process of review and evaluation of these maps at each stage.

The identification and selection of Units to be included in this document has been carried out by the NTO. The Core or Mandatory Units and Optional Units for the NVQs derived from these occupational standards are indicated on the back cover of this document. In some cases, all the necessary Units for the NVQ will be included, in others the NTO will have prioritised the most popular Units for inclusion.

National Curriculum	Literacy/Numeracy	Key Skills	National qualifications framework
		Key Skills Level 5	National qualifications framework Level 5
		Key Skills Level 4	National qualifications framework Level 4
		Key Skills Level 3	National qualifications framework Level 3
	Literacy/Numeracy Level 2	Key Skills Level 2	National qualifications framework Level 2
National Curriculum Level 5	Literacy/Numeracy Level 1	Key Skills Level 1	National qualifications framework Level 1
National Curriculum Level 4			
National Curriculum Level 3	Literacy/Numeracy Entry 3		
National Curriculum Level 2	Literacy/Numeracy Entry 2		Entry Level
National Curriculum Level 1	Literacy/Numeracy Entry 1		

2. Workplace basic skills

How many employees have difficulties with basic skills?

23% of people of working age have low levels of literacy and numeracy – almost 7 million people.

Fact

All countries have problems with poor literacy and numeracy, but the UK, when compared with other developed nations, has more problems than most – 23% with very low literacy skills in the UK, compared with 7% in Sweden and 12% in Germany.

Source: Adult Literacy in Britain, ONS

What does this mean in real numbers of employees?

Population of England	**49.3 million**
61.4% of working age (16-59/64)	**30.27 million**
23% of people of working age are likely to have 'very poor' basic skills	**6.96 million**

Source: Adult Literacy in Britain, ONS

It is a fact that in small and medium sized businesses, over 2 million workers are likely to have poor basic skills. In large organisations a further 2 million employees have difficulties with basic skills and in the public sector there are a million more workers with poor basic skills.

What are the consequences of poor basic skills amongst employees?

Workers with poor basic skills are at a considerable disadvantage in the workplace. Research has shown that employees with basic skills difficulties:

- will be less likely to receive work-related training;
- will have a limited number of jobs open to them;
- may find themselves vulnerable in times of change;
- often turn down promotion because they are afraid of the paperwork;
- will often be in lower paid jobs.

What are the consequences for employers?

Many of the problems experienced at work are linked to poor basic skills. Training, health and safety, quality procedures and many more issues are affected by employees who lack the skills to deal with the requirements of the workplace. Poor basic skills may mean:

- poor productivity;
- administration errors with customer orders;
- increased wastage rates;
- poor customer relations;

- incorrect production of orders;
- increased machine downtime;
- inefficiency of production or provision of services;
- increased staff turnover;
- difficulties over the introduction of new methods of working and new technology;
- external recruitment instead of internal promotion.

And what about the economy?

The Moser Report, *Improving literacy and numeracy – A fresh start,* published in 1999, suggested that poor basic skills might be one of the reasons for low productivity in the UK economy.

> *At work, basic skills matter crucially. They are a key to employability ... And there is evidence that they are growing in importance, employers rate them ever more highly. Moreover, poor basic skills affect the efficiency and competitiveness of the economy. The pace of development and change in business is undermined. They represent a significant cost to British industry.*

> A report, quoted by David Blunkett in 1997, suggested that poor literacy costs business and government £10 billion every year.
>
> Source: *Education and Training and their Impact on the Economy,* Ernst and Young

What are the benefits of providing training and improving the levels of basic skills amongst workers?

- Ability to improve performance and meet targets
- Increased efficiency and productivity
- Improved staff retention and commitment
- Improved staff take-up and benefit from training
- Ability to re-deploy staff
- Improved customer service
- Improved skills and confidence amongst workers
- Increased ability to perform jobs to national standards and achieve accreditation

3. Mapping rationale

How many Adult Literacy and Numeracy Standards are shown for each occupational standard of work?

The mapping has been carried out using a number of factors in order to decide the appropriate choice of Adult Literacy and Numeracy Standards. In collaboration with the NTO, we have decided on the **main**, or **critical**, basic skills required in order to perform each of the performance criteria or work standards.

In some cases, there will be only one Adult Literacy and Numeracy Standard mapped, for example, *Reading* in order to follow straightforward work instructions. For other performance criteria, more than one Adult Literacy and Numeracy Standard will be included in the map, for example, *Speaking and listening* and *Writing* will be shown when a worker has to make a report both verbally and in writing.

Which Adult Literacy and Numeracy Standard statements have been used and why?

As a general rule, in these maps the main purpose of the work standard has been the guiding factor in deciding which of the following basic skills statements is used.

Speaking and Listening

- *Speak to communicate* – if the main purpose of the task is to give information.
- *Listen and respond* – if the main purpose is to receive or gain information.
- *Engage in discussion* – in cases where there is a requirement to engage in an exchange of information.

Reading

- *Read and understand* – in instances when the worker needs to read a range of texts in order to gain understanding about concepts or principles.
- *Read and obtain information* – when the worker needs to follow a set of guidelines or written instructions in order to complete a task or procedure.

Writing

- *Write to communicate* – this statement covers all the occasions when a worker would need to write in order to perform a task. The appropriate descriptor would then apply eg information, ideas or opinions, depending on the context.

Numeracy

- *Understanding and using mathematical information* – this statement has generally been used to describe tasks where information, problems or instructions are given in numerical form (a product specification, product codes, charts and timetables).
- *Calculating and manipulating mathematical information* – is used when actual calculations have to be done and results are generated (calibrating a machine, weighing items, handling money).
- *Interpreting results and communicating mathematical information* – this is used when a task involves reporting or recording mathematical information (stock control sheets, quality data sheets).

Which level has been chosen and why?

Three levels from the Standards have been used in these maps.

- *Entry 3* – this level includes work tasks involving text, writing and numeracy in familiar and everyday contexts and of limited length.

- *Level 1* – this level has been chosen to describe the skills required to perform routine and straightforward work tasks of varying length.

- *Level 2* – this is used where tasks at work are more complex or non-routine.

4. Guidelines for use

How to use the grids

The basic skills grids provide an 'at-a-glance' overview of the range and levels of basic skills required for each unit. From this section you can move to the detailed information about basic skills in the maps, for the purposes of training or staff development. The diagram below illustrates how to use the grids.

Basic Skills Grid

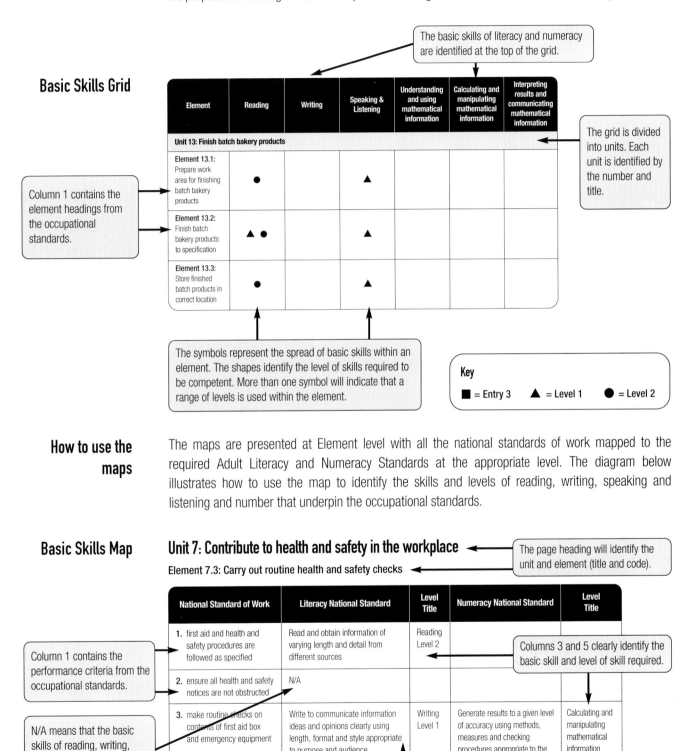

The basic skills of literacy and numeracy are identified at the top of the grid.

Element	Reading	Writing	Speaking & Listening	Understanding and using mathematical information	Calculating and manipulating mathematical information	Interpreting results and communicating mathematical information
Unit 13: Finish batch bakery products						
Element 13.1: Prepare work area for finishing batch bakery products	●		▲			
Element 13.2: Finish batch bakery products to specification	▲ ●		▲			
Element 13.3: Store finished batch products in correct location	●		▲			

The grid is divided into units. Each unit is identified by the number and title.

Column 1 contains the element headings from the occupational standards.

The symbols represent the spread of basic skills within an element. The shapes identify the level of skills required to be competent. More than one symbol will indicate that a range of levels is used within the element.

Key

■ = Entry 3   ▲ = Level 1   ● = Level 2

How to use the maps

The maps are presented at Element level with all the national standards of work mapped to the required Adult Literacy and Numeracy Standards at the appropriate level. The diagram below illustrates how to use the map to identify the skills and levels of reading, writing, speaking and listening and number that underpin the occupational standards.

Basic Skills Map

Unit 7: Contribute to health and safety in the workplace

The page heading will identify the unit and element (title and code).

Element 7.3: Carry out routine health and safety checks

National Standard of Work	Literacy National Standard	Level Title	Numeracy National Standard	Level Title
1. first aid and health and safety procedures are followed as specified	Read and obtain information of varying length and detail from different sources	Reading Level 2		
2. ensure all health and safety notices are not obstructed	N/A			
3. make routine checks on contents of first aid box and emergency equipment	Write to communicate information ideas and opinions clearly using length, format and style appropriate to purpose and audience	Writing Level 1	Generate results to a given level of accuracy using methods, measures and checking procedures appropriate to the specified purpose – use whole numbers – use common measures	Calculating and manipulating mathematical information Level 1

Column 1 contains the performance criteria from the occupational standards.

N/A means that the basic skills of reading, writing, speaking and listening and number are not applicable.

Columns 3 and 5 clearly identify the basic skill and level of skill required.

This column identifies the National Adult Literacy Standard required to be competent.

This column identifies the National Adult Numeracy Standard required to be competent.

Progression from the Adult Literacy and Numeracy Standards to the Adult Literacy and Numeracy Core Curriculum

In Sections 7 and 8 of this document you will find:

- an overview of the Adult Literacy and Numeracy Standards used in the maps;
- progression tables in speaking and listening, reading and writing, number, measures, shape and space and handling data.

The progression tables include:

- all the curriculum elements demonstrating the skills and knowledge required for teaching and learning;
- the curriculum references that lead you directly to the required part of the Adult Literacy and Numeracy Core Curriculum documents.

This diagram illustrates how the progression works.

Element 9.1: Process valid passenger tickets and passes

National Standard of Work	Literacy National Standard	Level Title	Numeracy National Standard	Level Title
1. confirm that the equipment used for processing tickets is in approved operational condition	N/A			
2. explain details of fares clearly to passengers in a manner that promotes understanding and goodwill	Speak to communicate information adapting speech and content to take account of the listener(s) and the medium	Speaking and Listening Level 1		
3. process fares in accordance . . .	Read and obtain information . . .	Reading Level 1	Generate results to a given level of accuracy . . .	

Actual page from curriculum

Speaking and listening

See also in the key skills: Communication key skills level 1
Part A: In discussions. . .
Part B: C1.1

LEVEL 1 At this level, adults can

listen and respond
to spoken language, including information and narratives, and follow explanations and instructions of varying lengths, adapting response to speaker, medium and context

speak to communicate
information, ideas and opinions adapting speech and content to take account of the listener(s) and medium

engage in discussion
with one or more people in familiar and unfamiliar situations, making clear and relevant contributions that respond to what others say and produce a shared understanding about different topics

in formal exchanges connected with education, training, work and social roles

Listen and respond   SLlr/L1

Skills, knowledge and understanding   Example

Adults should be taught to:

⑥ respond to questions on a range of topics
  – know that questions come in a variety of forms depending on context and topic
  – understand the expectations that different sorts of questions convey, and respond appropriately

Take part in an interview answering questions appropriately, to give a good account of their own experience and skills (e.g. for paid or voluntary work, or an education/training place).

Speak to communicate   SLc/L1

Skills, knowledge and understanding   Example

Adults should be taught to:

① speak clearly in a way which suits the situation
  – understand that pace, volume and precision of articulation vary depending on the situation (speaking face to face, on the telephone, to a group)

Speak clearly in a small team so as to be heard and understood, e.g. in a meeting to plan a street party.

5. Basic Skills Grids – Plant Maintenance

an overview of each Unit

Plant Maintenance

Element	Reading	Writing	Speaking & Listening	Understanding and using mathematical information	Calculating and manipulating mathematical information	Interpreting results and communicating mathematical information
Unit ERP 009: Shape engineering products by material removal using hand tools						
Element 1: Shape products to specification by manual removal of material	▲ ●			▲		
Element 2: Establish compliance with shaping specifications	▲ ●	▲	▲	▲	▲	
Unit ERP 037: Maintain the condition of engineering assets						
Element 1: Implement maintenance procedures for engineering assets	▲ ●	▲	▲		▲	
Element 2: Adjust engineering assets to meet operating requirements	▲ ●	▲			■	
Unit ERP 048: Reinstate the work area after engineering activities						
Element 1: Restore work areas	▲ ●	■	▲			
Element 2: Store resources for further use	▲ ●		▲			

Plant Maintenance

Element	Reading	Writing	Speaking & Listening	Understanding and using mathematical information	Calculating and manipulating mathematical information	Interpreting results and communicating mathematical information
Unit ERP 060: Contribute to minimising risks to life, property and the environment						
Element 1: Deal with hazards in the work environment	●	▲	▲			
Element 2: Minimise risks to life, property and the environment	●	▲	●			
Unit PR 14: Operate powered tools and equipment for routine and predictable requirements						
Element 1: Prepare powered tools and equipment for use	▲ ●	▲	▲			
Element 2: Run and operate powered tools and equipment	▲ ●	▲	▲			
Element 3: Shut down and carry out post-stop checks on powered tools and equipment	▲ ●	▲	▲			

Basic Skills Grids – Specialised Plant and Machinery Operations

an overview of each Unit

Specialised Plant and Machinery Operations

Key

■ = Entry 3   ▲ = Level 1   ● = Level 2

Element	Reading	Writing	Speaking & Listening	Understanding and using mathematical information	Calculating and manipulating mathematical information	Interpreting results and communicating mathematical information
Unit PR02: Contribute to health and safety in the workplace						
Element 1: Operate safely in the workplace	▲ ●		▲			
Element 2: Respond to emergencies	▲ ●	▲	▲			
Element 3: Assist in the security of the workplace	▲		▲			
Unit PR13: Assist in the efficiency of the workplace						
Element 1: Maintain a clean and tidy work station	▲ ●		▲			
Element 2: Maintain tools and equipment	●		▲			
Element 3: Organise your own work and maintain standards	▲ ●		▲ ●	■		

Specialised Plant and Machinery Operations

Element	Reading	Writing	Speaking & Listening	Understanding and using mathematical information	Calculating and manipulating mathematical information	Interpreting results and communicating mathematical information
Unit PR14: Operate powered tools and equipment for routine and predictable requirements						
Element 1: Prepare powered tools and equipment for use	▲ ●	▲	▲			
Element 2: Run and operate powered tools and equipment	▲ ●	▲	▲			
Element 3: Shut down and carry out post-stop checks on powered tools and equipment	▲ ●	▲	▲			
Unit PR15: Assist with the specified work activity						
Element 1: Receive information and instruction to assist the work activity	▲ ●		▲			
Element 2: Move and store materials and components to assist the work activity	▲ ●		▲			
Element 3: Assist the work activity to requirements	▲ ●		▲	▲		

Getting the basics right in Construction (Plant and Accessing)

Basic Skills Grids – Accessing Operations and Rigging

an overview of each Unit

Accessing Operations and Rigging

Key
■ = Entry 3   ▲ = Level 1   ● = Level 2

Element	Reading	Writing	Speaking & Listening	Understanding and using mathematical information	Calculating and manipulating mathematical information	Interpreting results and communicating mathematical information
Unit AR 01: Erect and dismantle general accessing equipment						
Element 1: Identify the requirement for general accessing equipment	▲ ●	▲	▲			
Element 2: Assemble general accessing equipment	▲ ●		▲		▲	
Element 3: Remove general accessing equipment	▲ ●	▲	▲			
Unit PR02: Contribute to health and safety in the workplace						
Element 1: Operate safely in the workplace	▲ ●		▲			
Element 2: Respond to emergencies	▲ ●	▲	▲			
Element 3: Assist in the security of the workplace	▲		▲			
Unit PR13: Assist in the efficiency of the workplace						
Element 1: Maintain a clean and tidy work station	▲ ●		▲			
Element 2: Maintain tools and equipment	●		▲			
Element 3: Organise your own work and maintain standards	▲ ●		▲ ●	■		

Accessing Operations and Rigging

Element	Reading	Writing	Speaking & Listening	Understanding and using mathematical information	Calculating and manipulating mathematical information	Interpreting results and communicating mathematical information
Unit PR 14: Operate powered tools and equipment for routine and predictable requirements						
Element 1: Prepare powered tools and equipment for use	▲ ●	▲	▲			
Element 2: Run and operate powered tools and equipment	▲ ●	▲	▲			
Element 3: Shut down and carry out post-stop checks on powered tools and equipment	▲ ●	▲	▲			
Unit PR15: Assist with the specified work activity						
Element 1: Receive information and instruction to assist the work activity	▲ ●		▲			
Element 2: Move and store materials and components to assist the work activity	▲ ●		▲			
Element 3: Assist the work activity to requirements	▲ ●		▲		▲	

Accessing Operations and Rigging

Element	Reading	Writing	Speaking & Listening	Understanding and using mathematical information	Calculating and manipulating mathematical information	Interpreting results and communicating mathematical information
Unit CR01: Set up protection and safety equipment for the working area (basic)						
Element 1: Install and maintain protection and safety equipment for the working area	▲ ●		▲			
Element 2: Remove protection and safety equipment from the working area	▲ ●		▲		▲	
Unit PR 07: Carry out slinging and signalling for the movement of loads						
Element 1: Prepare and sling loads for lifting	▲		▲ ●			
Element 2: Direct and control the movement and placing of loads	▲ ●		▲			

6. Basic Skills Maps – Plant Maintenance

detailed maps of the Performance Criteria in each Element

Unit ERP 009: Shape engineering products by material removal using hand tools

Element 1: Shape products to specification by manual removal of material

National Standard of Work	Literacy National Standard	Level Title	Numeracy National Standard	Level Title
1.1 the required product specification is obtained and is clear, current and complete	Read and obtain information from different sources.	Reading Level 1		
1.2 shaping techniques required are confirmed as suitable for specifications, and are used in accordance with operational procedures	Read and obtain information from different sources.	Reading Level 1	Read and understand straightforward mathematical information used for different purposes and independently select relevant information from given graphical, numerical and written material.	Understanding and using mathematical information Level 1
1.3 product shape produced is a correct interpretation of specifications	Read and obtain information from different sources.	Reading Level 1		
1.4 tools used during the shaping process are handled safely	N/A			
1.5 problems relating to the shaping process are dealt with promptly in line with approved guidelines for deciding what action to take	Read and obtain information from different sources.	Reading Level 1		
1.6 health and safety and other relevant legislation and guidelines are complied with at all times	Read and obtain information of varying length and detail from different sources.	Reading Level 2		

Unit ERP 009: Shape engineering products by material removal using hand tools

Element 2: Establish compliance with shaping specifications

National Standard of Work	Literacy National Standard	Level Title	Numeracy National Standard	Level Title
2.1 clear, current and complete details of the required specifications are available for reference	Read and obtain information from different sources.	Reading Level 1		
2.2 all aspects cited in specifications are adequately checked for compliance	Read and obtain information from different sources.	Reading Level 1	Read and understand mathematical information used for different purposes and independently select and compare relevant information from a variety of graphical, numerical and written material. Generate results to a given level of accuracy using methods, measures and checking procedures appropriate to the specified purpose – use common measures – use space and shape.	Understanding and using mathematical information Level 1 Calculating and manipulating mathematical information Level 1
2.3 suitable equipment and methods are selected and used to check compliance	Read and obtain information from different sources.			
2.4 an accurate assessment of compliance is made with defects and variations correctly identified				
2.5 defects and variations are dealt with promptly in accordance with approved guidelines for deciding what action to take	Speak to communicate information, ideas and opinions adapting speech and content to take account of the listener(s) and medium.	Speaking and Listening Level 1		
2.6 records of the checks and assessments made are current, clear and accessible to authorised personnel	Write to communicate information, ideas and opinions clearly using length, format and style appropriate to purpose and audience.	Writing Level 1		
2.7 health and safety and other relevant legislation and guidelines are complied with at all times	Read and obtain information of varying length and detail from different sources.	Reading Level 2		

Unit ERP 037: Maintain the condition of engineering assets

Element 1: Implement maintenance procedures for engineering assets

National Standard of Work	Literacy National Standard	Level Title	Numeracy National Standard	Level Title
1.1 relevant authorisation procedures, safe working practice details and specific instructions are obtained and complied with	Read and obtain information of varying length and detail from different sources.	Reading Level 2		
1.2 maintenance is completed in an agreed timescale, using safe and appropriate methods and in line with agreed procedures	Read and obtain information from different sources.	Reading Level 1	Generate results to a given level of accuracy using methods, measures and checking procedures appropriate to the specified purpose – use common measures.	Calculating and manipulating mathematical information Level 1
1.3 actions are completed in the order as defined in procedures	Read and obtain information from different sources.	Reading Level 1		
1.4 resources are used cost-effectively	N/A			
1.5 required records are complete, accurate and up to date	Write to communicate information, ideas and opinions clearly using length, format and style appropriate to purpose and audience.	Writing Level 1		
1.6 difficulties in implementing procedures as specified are reported promptly and accurately to the relevant parties	Speak to communicate information, ideas and opinions adapting speech and content to take account of the listener(s) and medium.	Speaking and Listening Level 1		
1.7 health and safety and other relevant legislation and guidelines are complied with at all times	Read and obtain information of varying length and detail from different sources.	Reading Level 2		

Unit ERP 037: Maintain the condition of engineering assets

Element 2: Adjust engineering assets to meet operating requirements

National Standard of Work	Literacy National Standard	Level Title	Numeracy National Standard	Level Title
2.1 operating requirements are obtained and are available for reference	Read and obtain information from different sources.	Reading Level 1		
2.2 adjusted assets comply with specified operating requirements	Read and obtain information from different sources.	Reading Level 1		
2.3 adjustment is carried out within required timescales, with minimum disruption to any ongoing activities			Generate results to a given level of accuracy using given methods, measures and checking procedures appropriate to the specified purpose – use common measures.	Calculating and manipulating mathematical information Entry 3
2.4 adjustments are made using the specified tools, materials and methods			Generate results to a given level of accuracy using given methods, measures and checking procedures appropriate to the specified purpose – use common measures.	Calculating and manipulating mathematical information Entry 3
2.5 achievement of requirements is monitored accurately and the results accurately recorded and taken into account in achieving compliance with requirements	Write to communicate information, ideas and opinions clearly using length, format and style appropriate to purpose and audience. Read and obtain information from different sources.	Writing Level 1 Reading Level 1		
2.6 assets failing to meet the required performance after adjustment are identified and details recorded for further action	Write to communicate information, ideas and opinions clearly using length, format and style appropriate to purpose and audience. Read and obtain information from different sources.	Writing Level 1 Reading Level 1		
2.7 health and safety and other relevant legislation and guidelines are complied with at all times	Read and obtain information of varying length and detail from different sources.	Reading Level 2		

Unit ERP 048: Reinstate the work area after engineering activities

Element 1: Restore work areas

National Standard of Work	Literacy National Standard	Level Title	Numeracy National Standard	Level Title
1.1 work area is restored according to agreed requirements and schedules	Listen and respond to spoken language, including information and narratives, and follow explanations and instructions of varying length, adapting response to speaker, medium and context. Read and obtain information from different sources.	Speaking and Listening Level 1 Reading Level 1		
1.2 requirements of uses of the work area are satisfied wherever possible	Read and obtain information from different sources.	Reading Level 1		
1.3 equipment, components and materials that can be re-used are separated out from waste for appropriate treatment	N/A			
1.4 waste materials are stored in an appropriate manner prior to disposal and its contents clearly identified	Write to communicate information and opinions with some adaptation to the intended audience.	Writing Entry 3		
1.5 waste materials are disposed of in a safe manner and by the appropriate methods	N/A			
1.6 problems in restoring the work area are identified and appropriate remedial action promptly taken	Speak to communicate information, ideas and opinions adapting speech and content to take account of the listener(s) and medium.	Speaking and Listening Level 1		
1.7 health and safety and other relevant legislation and guidelines are complied with at all times	Read and obtain information of varying length and detail from different sources.	Reading Level 2		

Unit ERP 048: Reinstate the work area after engineering activities

Element 2: Store resources for further use

National Standard of Work	Literacy National Standard	Level Title	Numeracy National Standard	Level Title
2.1 storage is carried out in accordance with specified storage procedures	Read and obtain information from different sources.	Reading Level 1		
2.2 resources are stored using the correct safe handling techniques	Read and obtain information from different sources.	Reading Level 1		
2.3 resources are stored according to specifications and control schedules	Read and obtain information from different sources.	Reading Level 1		
2.4 resources are stored in the correct position for further use	N/A			
2.5 all unnecessary packaging and equipment is removed after storage and disposed of safely	N/A			
2.6 problems with the storing process are promptly identified and the appropriate action taken to overcome them	Speak to communicate information, ideas and opinions adapting speech and content to take account of the listener(s) and medium.	Speaking and Listening Level 1		
2.7 health and safety and other relevant legislation and guidelines are complied with at all times	Read and obtain information of varying length and detail from different sources.	Reading Level 2		

Unit ERP 060: Contribute to minimising risks to life, property and the environment

Element 1: Deal with hazards in the work environment

National Standard of Work	Literacy National Standard	Level Title	Numeracy National Standard	Level Title
1.1 checking for hazards is undertaken in line with procedures and criteria specified	Read and obtain information of varying length and detail from different sources.	Reading Level 2		
1.2 hazards are accurately identified and acted upon according to specified guidelines	Read and obtain information of varying length and detail from different sources.	Reading Level 2		
1.3 immediate action is taken with situations which pose an imminent threat and a report subsequently made to the appropriate authorised person	Speak to communicate information, ideas and opinions adapting speech and content to take account of the listener(s) and medium. Write to communicate information, ideas and opinions clearly using length, format and style appropriate to purpose and audience.	Speaking and Listening Level 1 Writing Level 1		
1.4 hazards identified and actions taken are recorded clearly and accurately in line with relevant control requirements	Write to communicate information, ideas and opinions clearly using length, format and style appropriate to purpose and audience.	Writing Level 1		

Getting the basics right in Construction (Plant and Accessing)

Unit ERP 060: Contribute to minimising risks to life, property and the environment

Element 2: Minimise risks to life, property and the environment

National Standard of Work	Literacy National Standard	Level Title	Numeracy National Standard	Level Title
2.1 measures to minimise risk are put into action with a priority and timescale that are in line with the overall organisational risk control strategy	Read and obtain information of varying length and detail from different sources.	Reading Level 2		
2.2 any people affected are informed clearly and concisely of the risk control measures in place and are given opportunities to clarify any implications for them	Engage in discussion with one or more people in a variety of different situations, making clear and effective contributions that produce outcomes appropriate to purpose and topic.	Speaking and Listening level 2		
2.3 health and safety and other relevant legislation and guidelines are complied with at all times	Read and obtain information of varying length and detail from different sources.	Reading Level 2		
2.4 information provided for organisational safety system records is clear, accurate and up to date	Write to communicate information, ideas and opinions clearly using length, format and style appropriate to purpose and audience.	Writing Level 1		
2.5 where requested by authorised personnel, the effectiveness of risk control measures is monitored and additional action taken promptly where needed	Listen and respond to spoken language, including information and narratives, and follow explanations and instructions of varying length, adapting response to speaker, medium and context.	Speaking and Listening Level 1		

Unit PR 14: Operate powered tools and equipment for routine and predictable requirements

Element 1: Prepare powered tools and equipment for use

National Standard of Work	Literacy National Standard	Level Title	Numeracy National Standard	Level Title
1.1 operations requiring the use of powered tools and equipment are identified and confirmed in accordance with the specifications and work instructions	Read and obtain information from different sources. Listen and respond to spoken language, including information and narratives, and follow explanations and instructions of varying length, adapting response to speaker, medium and context.	Reading Level 1 Speaking and Listening Level 1		
1.2 pre-start inspections are carried out on the powered tools and equipment in accordance with approved procedures and practices	Read and obtain information from different sources.	Reading Level 1		
1.3 any defect(s) of the powered tools and equipment are identified, recorded and appropriate action taken to correct them	Speak to communicate information, ideas and opinions adapting speech and content to take account of the listener(s) and medium. Write to communicate information, ideas and opinions clearly using length, format and style appropriate to purpose and audience.	Speaking and Listening Level 1 Writing Level 1		
1.4 powered tools and equipment are confirmed safe, correct and ready for use in accordance with the work requirements and approved procedures and practices	Speak to communicate information, ideas and opinions adapting speech and content to take account of the listener(s) medium. Read and obtain information from different sources.	Speaking and Listening Level 1 Reading Level 1		
1.5 problems and conditions outside the responsibility of the candidate are referred to an authorised person	Speak to communicate information, ideas and opinions adapting speech and content to take account of the listener(s) and medium.	Speaking and Listening Level 1		
1.6 work is carried out to approved procedures and practices and in compliance with statutory requirements	Read and obtain information of varying length and detail from different sources.	Reading Level 2		

Unit PR 14: Operate powered tools and equipment for routine and predictable requirements

Element 2: Run and operate powered tools and equipment

National Standard of Work	Literacy National Standard	Level Title	Numeracy National Standard	Level Title
2.1 start and stop procedures carried out to confirm functions are in accordance with safe control and the manufacturer's operating instructions	Read and obtain information of varying length and detail from different sources.	Reading Level 2		
2.2 powered tools and equipment are run and operated to the work requirement	Read and obtain information from different sources.	Reading Level 1		
2.3 operations are carried out safely in accordance with specifications and approved procedures and practices	Read and obtain information from different sources.	Reading Level 1		
2.4 defects in performance are identified, recorded and reported to the appropriate person(s)	Speak to communicate information, ideas and opinions adapting speech and content to take account of the listener(s) and medium. Write to communicate information, ideas and opinions clearly using length, format and style appropriate to purpose and audience.	Speaking and Listening Level 1 Writing Level 1		
2.5 problems and conditions outside the responsibility of the candidate are referred to an authorised person	Speak to communicate information, ideas and opinions adapting speech and content to take account of the listener(s) and medium.	Speaking and Listening Level 1		
2.6 work is carried out to approved procedures and practices and in compliance with statutory requirements	Read and obtain information of varying length and detail from different sources.	Reading Level 2		

Unit PR 14: Operate powered tools and equipment for routine and predictable requirements

Element 3: Shut down and carry out post-stop checks on powered tools and equipment

National Standard of Work	Literacy National Standard	Level Title	Numeracy National Standard	Level Title
3.1 powered tools and equipment are stopped safely in accordance with approved procedures and practices	Read and obtain information from different sources.	Reading Level 1		
3.2 post-stop checks are carried out in accordance with organisational and operational procedure	Read and obtain information from different sources.	Reading Level 1		
3.3 defects and replacement needs are identified, recorded and reported to the appropriate person(s)	Speak to communicate information, ideas and opinions adapting speech and content to take account of the listener(s) and medium. Write to communicate information, ideas and opinions clearly using length, format and style appropriate to purpose and audience.	Speaking and Listening Level 1 Writing Level 1		
3.4 powered tools and equipment are left safe and secure in accordance with approved procedures and practices	Read and obtain information from different sources.	Reading Level 1		
3.5 problems and conditions outside the responsibility of the candidate are referred to an authorised person	Speak to communicate information, ideas and opinions adapting speech and content to take account of the listener(s) and medium.	Speaking and Listening Level 1		
3.6 work is carried out to approved procedures and practices and in compliance with statutory requirements	Read and obtain information of varying length and detail from different sources.	Reading Level 2		

Basic Skills Maps — Specialised Plant and Machinery Operations

detailed maps of the Performance Criteria in each Element

Unit PR02: Contribute to health and safety in the workplace

Element 1: Operate safely in the workplace

National Standard of Work	Literacy National Standard	Level Title	Numeracy National Standard	Level Title
1.1 work activities are carried out safely to avoid creating hazardous situations that may endanger operators of the work and other personnel	Read and obtain information of varying length and detail from different sources.	Reading Level 2		
1.2 hazards and potential hazards identified in the workplace are dealt with appropriately within the responsibility and capability of the work operator and reported promptly to the appropriate person(s)	Speak to communicate information, ideas and opinions adapting speech and content to take account of the listener(s) and medium Read and obtain information from different sources.	Speaking and Listening Level 1 Reading Level 1		
1.3 communications are clear and information or instruction is confirmed as understood	Speak to communicate information, ideas and opinions adapting speech and content to take account of the listener(s) and medium	Speaking and Listening Level 1		
1.4 all tools and equipment are used safely in accordance with organisational procedures, manufacturer's instructions and relevant statutory regulations	Read and obtain information of varying length and detail from different sources.	Reading Level 2		
1.5 work materials and components are handled and stored in accordance with approved procedures and practices	Read and obtain information from different sources.	Reading Level 1		
1.6 manual handling is carried out safely using appropriate handling techniques	Read and obtain information from different sources.	Reading Level 1		
1.7 accident(s) and incident(s) are reported promptly to an authorised person in accordance with approved procedures and practices	Speak to communicate information, ideas and opinions adapting speech and content to take account of the listener(s) and medium. Read and obtain information of varying length and detail from different sources.	Speaking and Listening Level 1 Reading Level 2		

Getting the basics right in Construction (Plant and Accessing)

National Standard of Work	Literacy National Standard	Level Title	Numeracy National Standard	Level Title
1.8 appropriate personal protective equipment is used in compliance with safe working practices	Read and obtain information from different sources.	Reading Level 1		
1.9 work is carried out to approved procedures and practices and in compliance with statutory requirements	Read and obtain information of varying length and detail from different sources.	Reading Level 2		

Unit PR02: Contribute to health and safety in the workplace

Element 2: Respond to emergencies

National Standard of Work	Literacy National Standard	Level Title	Numeracy National Standard	Level Title
2.1 in the event of an emergency, procedures are implemented promptly and correctly in accordance with recognised safe practice and organisational policy	Read and obtain information of varying length and detail from different sources.	Reading Level 2		
2.2 accident(s) and incident(s) are responded to within the responsibility and capability of the work operator and promptly reported to an authorised person	Read and obtain information from different sources. Speak to communicate information, ideas and opinions adapting speech and content to take account of the listener(s) and medium.	Reading Level 1 Speaking and Listening Level 1		
2.3 use of emergency appliances is carried out in accordance with approved procedures and practices	Read and obtain information from different sources.	Reading Level 1		
2.4 details of accident(s) and incident(s) are recorded in accordance with approved procedures and practices	Write to communicate information, ideas and opinions clearly using length, format and style appropriate to purpose and audience.	Writing Level 1		
2.5 problems and conditions outside the responsibility of the job holder are referred to an authorised person	Speak to communicate information, ideas and opinions adapting speech and content to take account of the listener(s) and medium.	Speaking and Listening Level 1		

Unit PRO2: Contribute to health and safety in the workplace

Element 3: Assist in the security of the workplace

National Standard of Work	Literacy National Standard	Level Title	Numeracy National Standard	Level Title
3.1 unauthorised personnel seen in the workplace are dealt with in accordance with organisational procedures and the appropriate person(s) advised	Read and obtain information from different sources. Speak to communicate information, ideas and opinions adapting speech and content to take account of the listener(s) medium.	Reading Level 1 Speaking and Listening Level 1		
3.2 arrangements for security are observed and maintained in accordance with approved procedures and practices	Read and obtain information from different sources.	Reading Level 1		
3.3 potential risks to security are reported promptly to the appropriate person(s) and remedial action taken as necessary in accordance with organisational procedures	Speak to communicate information, ideas and opinions adapting speech and content to take account of the listener(s) and medium.	Speaking and Listening Level 1		
3.4 breaches of security are reported immediately to an authorised person	Read and obtain information from different sources.	Reading Level 1		
3.5 problems and conditions outside the responsibility of the job holder are referred to an authorised person	Speak to communicate information, ideas and opinions adapting speech and content to take account of the listener(s) and medium.	Speaking and Listening Level 1		

Unit PR13: Assist in the efficiency of the workplace

Element 1: Maintain a clean and tidy work station

National Standard of Work	Literacy National Standard	Level Title	Numeracy National Standard	Level Title
1.1 the work station is maintained clean and tidy so that it complements the work activity and the surrounding environment	N/A			
1.2 waste and debris are disposed of in designated receptacles or locations in accordance with instruction and approved procedures and practices	Listen and respond to spoken language, including information and narratives, and follow explanations and instructions of varying length, adapting response to speaker, medium and context. Read and obtain information from different sources.	Speaking and Listening Level 1 Reading Level 1		
1.3 work tools and equipment not in use are stored and housed safely in the designated place	N/A			
1.4 work materials and components are stored in accordance with approved procedures and practices	Read and obtain information from different sources.	Reading Level 1		
1.5 harmful materials are removed or reported to an authorised person for further action	Speak to communicate information, ideas and opinions adapting speech and content to take account of the listener(s) and medium.	Speaking and Listening Level 1		
1.6 problems and conditions outside the responsibility of the job holder are referred to an authorised person	Speak to communicate information, ideas and opinions adapting speech and content to take account of the listener(s) and medium.	Speaking and Listening Level 1		
1.7 work is carried out to approved procedures and practices and in compliance with statutory requirements	Read and obtain information of varying length and detail from different sources.	Reading Level 2		

Unit PR13: Assist in the efficiency of the workplace

Element 2: Maintain tools and equipment

National Standard of Work	Literacy National Standard	Level Title	Numeracy National Standard	Level Title
2.1 tools and equipment are maintained in a clean and usable condition	N/A			
2.2 powered equipment is shut down and isolated from the power source prior to any maintenance	N/A			
2.3 equipment is maintained in accordance with the manufacturers' recommendations	Read and obtain information of varying length and detail from different sources.	Reading Level 2		
2.4 tools and equipment are confirmed as operational and safe for use	Speak to communicate information, ideas and opinions adapting speech and content to take account of the listener(s) and medium.	Speaking and Listening Level 1		
2.5 damage to tools and equipment is reported to an authorised person	Speak to communicate information, ideas and opinions adapting speech and content to take account of the listener(s) and medium.	Speaking and Listening Level 1		
2.6 problems and conditions outside the responsibility of the job holder are referred to an authorised person	Speak to communicate information, ideas and opinions adapting speech and content to take account of the listener(s) and medium.	Speaking and Listening Level 1		
2.7 work is carried out to approved procedures and practices and in compliance with statutory requirements	Read and obtain information of varying length and detail from different sources.	Reading Level 2		

Unit PR13: Assist in the efficiency of the workplace

Element 3: Organise your own work and maintain standards

National Standard of Work	Literacy National Standard	Level Title	Numeracy National Standard	Level Title
3.1 work is organised to comply with instructions and the agreed schedules	Listen and respond to spoken language, including information and narratives, and follow explanations and instructions of varying length, adapting response to speaker, medium and context. Read and obtain information from different sources.	Speaking and Listening Level 1 Reading Level 1	Read and understand information given by numbers, symbols, diagrams and charts used for different purposes and in different ways in graphical, numerical and written material.	Understanding and using mathematical information Entry 3
3.2 work methods are employed in accordance with approved procedures and practices and optimise the use of time	Read and obtain information from different sources.	Reading Level 1		
3.3 your own work is co-ordinated with other relevant personnel and related activities as required	Engage in discussion with one or more people in familiar and unfamiliar situations, making clear and relevant contributions that respond to what others say and produce a shared understanding about different topics.	Speaking and Listening Level 1		
3.4 any suggestions for improvements to work methods are referred to an authorised person for confirmation and agreement on the action to be taken	Speak to communicate straightforward and detailed information, ideas and opinions clearly, adapting speech and content to take account of the listener(s), medium, purpose and situation.	Speaking and Listening Level 2		
3.5 work is done to the agreed standards and is in accordance with the specification and the organisational policy	Read and obtain information from different sources.	Reading Level 1		
3.6 deviations in standard or specification are agreed with an authorised person	Speak to communicate information, ideas and opinions adapting speech and content to take account of the listener(s) and medium.	Speaking and Listening Level 1		

National Standard of Work	Literacy National Standard	Level Title	Numeracy National Standard	Level Title
3.7 work that may be detrimental to safety or the environment is referred to the appropriate person(s) in accordance with organisational and operational procedures	Speak to communicate information, ideas and opinions adapting speech and content to take account of the listener(s) and medium. Read and obtain information from different sources.	Speaking and Listening Level 1 Reading Level 1		
3.8 waste and debris are removed and disposed of in accordance with approved procedures and practices	Read and obtain information from different sources.	Reading Level 1		
3.9 work is carried out to approved procedures and practices and in compliance with statutory requirements	Read and obtain information of varying length and detail from different sources.	Reading Level 2		

Unit PR14: Operate powered tools and equipment for routine and predictable requirements

Element 1: Prepare powered tools and equipment for use

National Standard of Work	Literacy National Standard	Level Title	Numeracy National Standard	Level Title
1.1 operations requiring the use of powered tools and equipment are identified and confirmed in accordance with the specifications and work instructions	Read and obtain information from different sources. Listen and respond to spoken language, including information and narratives, and follow explanations and instructions of varying length, adapting response to speaker, medium and context.	Reading Level 1 Speaking and Listening Level 1		
1.2 pre-start inspections are carried out on the powered tools and equipment in accordance with approved procedures and practices	Read and obtain information from different sources.	Reading Level 1		
1.3 any defect(s) of the powered tools and equipment are identified, recorded and appropriate action taken to correct them	Speak to communicate information, ideas and opinions adapting speech and content to take account of the listener(s) and medium. Write to communicate information, ideas and opinions clearly using length, format and style appropriate to purpose and audience.	Speaking and Listening Level 1 Writing Level 1		
1.4 powered tools and equipment are confirmed safe, correct and ready for use in accordance with the work requirements and approved procedures and practices	Speak to communicate information, ideas and opinions adapting speech and content to take account of the listener(s) and medium. Read and obtain information from different sources.	Speaking and Listening Level 1 Reading Level 1		
1.5 problems and conditions outside the responsibility of the candidate are referred to an authorised person	Speak to communicate information, ideas and opinions adapting speech and content to take account of the listener(s) and medium.	Speaking and Listening Level 1		
1.6 work is carried out to approved procedures and practices and in compliance with statutory requirements	Read and obtain information of varying length and detail from different sources.	Reading Level 2		

Unit PR14: Operate powered tools and equipment for routine and predictable requirements

Element 2: Run and operate powered tools and equipment

National Standard of Work	Literacy National Standard	Level Title	Numeracy National Standard	Level Title
2.1 start and stop procedures are carried out to confirm functions are in accordance with safe control and the manufacturer's operating instructions	Read and obtain information of varying length and detail from different sources.	Reading Level 2		
2.2 powered tools and equipment are run and operated to the work requirement	Read and obtain information from different sources.	Reading Level 1		
2.3 operations are carried out safely in accordance with specifications and approved procedures and practices	Read and obtain information from different sources.	Reading Level 1		
2.4 defects in performance are identified, recorded and reported to the appropriate person(s)	Speak to communicate information, ideas and opinions adapting speech and content to take account of the listener(s) and medium. Write to communicate information, ideas and opinions clearly using length, format and style appropriate to purpose and audience.	Speaking and Listening Level 1 Writing Level 1		
2.5 problems and conditions outside the responsibility of the candidate are referred to an authorised person	Speak to communicate information, ideas and opinions adapting speech and content to take account of the listener(s) and medium.	Speaking and Listening Level 1		
2.6 work is carried out to approved procedures and practices and in compliance with statutory requirements	Read and obtain information of varying length and detail from different sources.	Reading Level 2		

Unit PR14: Operate powered tools and equipment for routine and predictable requirements

Element 3: Shut down and carry out post-stop checks on powered tools and equipment

National Standard of Work	Literacy National Standard	Level Title	Numeracy National Standard	Level Title
3.1 powered tools and equipment are stopped safely in accordance with approved procedures and practices	Read and obtain information from different sources.	Reading Level 1		
3.2 post-stop checks are carried out in accordance with organisational and operational procedures	Read and obtain information from different sources.	Reading Level 1		
3.3 defects and replacement needs are identified, recorded and reported to the appropriate person(s)	Speak to communicate information, ideas and opinions adapting speech and content to take account of the listener(s) medium. Write to communicate information, ideas and opinions clearly using length, format and style appropriate to purpose and audience.	Speaking and Listening Level 1 Writing Level 1		
3.4 powered tools and equipment are left safe and secure in accordance with approved procedures and practices	Read and obtain information from different sources.	Reading Level 1		
3.5 problems and conditions outside the responsibility of the candidate are referred to an authorised person	Speak to communicate information, ideas and opinions adapting speech and content to take account of the listener(s) and medium.	Speaking and Listening Level 1		
3.6 work is carried out to approved procedures and practices and in compliance with statutory requirements	Read and obtain information of varying length and detail from different sources.	Reading Level 2		

Unit PR15: Assist with the specified work activity

Element 1: Receive information and instruction to assist the work activity

National Standard of Work	Literacy National Standard	Level Title	Numeracy National Standard	Level Title
1.1 receive and confirm the understanding of information and instruction for the work activity	Listen and respond to spoken language, including information and narratives, and follow explanations and instructions of varying length, adapting response to speaker, medium and context. Read and obtain information from different sources.	Speaking and Listening Level 1 Reading Level 1		
1.2 circumstances of the work activity and its environment that differ from and are not compatible with the information and instruction are reported and referred to an authorised person	Speak to communicate information, ideas and opinions adapting speech and content to take account of the listener(s) and medium. Read and obtain information from different sources.	Speaking and Listening Level 1 Reading Level 1		
1.3 amendment and changes to information and instruction are confirmed and agreed with the appropriate person(s) in accordance with approved procedures and practices	Speak to communicate information, ideas and opinions adapting speech and content to take account of the listener(s) and medium. Read and obtain information from different sources.	Speaking and Listening Level 1 Reading Level 1		
1.4 where information is unclear, safety is not compromised and further clarification of information and instruction is sought	Engage in discussion with one or more people in familiar and unfamiliar situations, making clear and relevant contributions that respond to what others say and produce a shared understanding about different topics.	Speaking and Listening Level 1		
1.5 work is carried out to approved procedures and practices and in compliance with statutory requirements	Read and obtain information of varying length and detail from different sources.	Reading Level 2		

Unit PR15: Assist with the specified work activity

Element 2: Move and store materials and components to assist the work activity

National Standard of Work	Literacy National Standard	Level Title	Numeracy National Standard	Level Title
2.1 moving and storing of materials and components is carried out safely to instruction and the work requirements	Listen and respond to spoken language, including information and narratives, and follow explanations and instructions of varying length, adapting response to speaker, medium and context.	Speaking and Listening Level 1		
	Read and obtain information from different sources.	Reading Level 1		
2.2 hazardous materials and components are identified, made safe or removed in accordance with approved procedures and practices	Read and obtain information from different sources.	Reading Level 1		
2.3 movement of materials and components is carried out without endangering the work operator or others in accordance with approved procedures and practices	Read and obtain information from different sources.	Reading Level 1		
2.4 waste and harmful materials are disposed of in a manner that minimises danger to the environment in accordance with approved procedures and practices	Read and obtain information from different sources.	Reading Level 1		
2.5 the work area is tidily maintained in accordance with customer and organisational requirements	Read and obtain information from different sources.	Reading Level 1		

National Standard of Work	Literacy National Standard	Level Title	Numeracy National Standard	Level Title
2.6 problems and conditions outside the responsibility of the candidate are referred to the authorised person	Speak to communicate information, ideas and opinions adapting speech and content to take account of the listener(s) and medium.	Speaking and Listening Level 1		
2.7 work is carried out to approved procedures and practices and in compliance with statutory requirements	Read and obtain information of varying length and detail from different sources.	Reading Level 2		

Unit PR15: Assist with the specified work activity

Element 3: Assist the work activity to requirements

National Standard of Work	Literacy National Standard	Level Title	Numeracy National Standard	Level Title
3.1 assistance with the work activity is carried out to instruction and in accordance with requirements	Listen and respond to spoken language, including information and narratives, and follow explanations and instructions of varying length, adapting response to speaker, medium and context.	Speaking and Listening Level 1	Generate results to a given level of accuracy using methods, measures and checking procedures appropriate to the specified purpose – use whole numbers – use common measures.	Calculating and manipulating mathematical information Level 1
3.2 work done is to the required standards and specification of the work requirement	Read and obtain information from different sources.	Reading Level 1		
3.3 tools and equipment used with the work activity are safe and in accordance with the approved procedures and practices	Read and obtain information from different sources.	Reading Level 1		
3.4 work is carried out in a manner to help minimise damage and disruption to the surrounding environment	N/A			
3.5 problems and conditions outside the responsibility of the candidate are referred to the authorised person	Speak to communicate information, ideas and opinions adapting speech and content to take account of the listener(s) and medium.	Speaking and Listening Level 1		
3.6 work is carried out to approved procedures and practices and in compliance with statutory requirements	Read and obtain information of varying length and detail from different sources.	Reading Level 2		

Basic Skills Maps – Accessing Operations and Rigging

detailed maps of the Performance Criteria in each Element

Unit AR 01: Erect and dismantle general accessing equipment

Element 1: Identify the requirement for general accessing equipment

National Standard of Work	Literacy National Standard	Level Title	Numeracy National Standard	Level Title
1.1 the requirement for general accessing equipment is identified in accordance with the work to be done according to instructions and information given	Listen and respond to spoken language, including information and narratives, and follow explanations and instructions of varying length, adapting response to speaker, medium and context. Read and obtain information from different sources.	Speaking and Listening Level 1 Reading Level 1		
1.2 the area and position for the accessing equipment is identified and the extent of the requirements confirmed	Speak to communicate information, ideas and opinions adapting speech and content to take account of the listener(s) and medium.	Speaking and Listening Level 1		
1.3 any change from information and instructions relating to the requirements is communicated with the appropriate persons	Speak to communicate information, ideas and opinions adapting speech and content to take account of the listener(s) and medium.	Speaking and Listening Level 1		
1.4 the access equipment is obtained and confirmed suitable and safe for the work requirement	Speak to communicate information, ideas and opinions adapting speech and content to take account of the listener(s) and medium. Read and obtain information from different sources.	Speaking and Listening Level 1 Reading Level 1		
1.5 tools and fixing aids are obtained to erect and secure the accessing equipment as appropriate to the work requirements	Read and obtain information from different sources.	Reading Level 1		
1.6 documentation to obtain and use access equipment is maintained in accordance with operational and organisation requirements	Write to communicate information, ideas and opinions clearly using length, format and style appropriate to purpose and audience.	Writing Level 1		

National Standard of Work	Literacy National Standard	Level Title	Numeracy National Standard	Level Title
1.7 problems and conditions outside the responsibility of the job holder are referred to an authorised person	Speak to communicate information, ideas and opinions adapting speech and content to take account of the listener(s) and medium.	Speaking and Listening Level 1		
1.9 work is carried out to approved procedures and practices and in compliance with statutory requirements	Read and obtain information of varying length and detail from different sources.	Reading Level 2		

Unit AR 01: Erect and dismantle general accessing equipment

Element 2: Assemble general accessing equipment

National Standard of Work	Literacy National Standard	Level Title	Numeracy National Standard	Level Title
2.1 general accessing equipment is positioned and erected to the work requirement in accordance with approved procedures and practices	Read and obtain information from different sources.	Reading Level 1	Generate results to a given level of accuracy using methods, measures and checking procedures appropriate to the specified purpose.	Calculate and manipulate mathematical information Level 1
2.2 defective and damaged accessing equipment is identified and corrected as appropriate in accordance with operational and organisational procedures	Read and obtain information from different sources.	Reading Level 1	Generate results to a given level of accuracy using methods, measures and checking procedures appropriate to the specified purpose.	Calculate and manipulate mathematical information Level 1
2.3 erection and positioning of the accessing equipment is carried out with due consideration to the surrounding environment and safety for others	N/A			
2.4 accessing equipment is confirmed secure and appropriate to the operational requirement	Read and obtain information from different sources. Speak to communicate information, ideas and opinions adapting speech and content to take account of the listener(s) and medium.	Reading Level 1 Speaking and Listening Level 1		
2.5 fixing aids are used to ensure the security and safety of the accessing equipment in accordance with operational requirements and approved procedures and practices	Read and obtain information from different sources.	Reading Level 1		
2.6 problems and conditions outside the responsibility of the job holder are referred to an authorised person	Speak to communicate information, ideas and opinions adapting speech and content to take account of the listener(s) and medium.	Speaking and Listening Level 1		

National Standard of Work	Literacy National Standard	Level Title	Numeracy National Standard	Level Title
2.7 work is carried out to approved procedures and practices and in compliance with statutory requirements	Read and obtain information of varying length and detail from different sources.	Reading Level 2		

Unit AR 01: Erect and dismantle general accessing equipment

Element 3: Remove general accessing equipment

National Standard of Work	Literacy National Standard	Level Title	Numeracy National Standard	Level Title
3.1 on completion of work, general accessing equipment is dismantled and removed in accordance with approved procedures and practices	Read and obtain information from different sources.	Reading Level 1		
3.2 dismantling the accessing equipment is carried out safely with due consideration to the surrounding environment and safety for others	N/A			
3.3 the accessing equipment is checked, stored and secured in accordance with the operational and organisational procedures	Read and obtain information from different sources.	Reading Level 1		
3.4 defective and damaged equipment is identified and reported to the appropriate persons in accordance with operational and organisational procedures	Speak to communicate information, ideas and opinions adapting speech and content to take account of the listener(s) and medium. Read and obtain information from different sources.	Speaking and listening Level 1 Reading Level 1		
3.5 documentation is maintained in accordance with operational and organisational requirements	Write to communicate information, ideas and opinions clearly using length, format and style appropriate to purpose and audience. Read and obtain information from different sources.	Writing Level 1 Reading Level 1		
3.6 problems and conditions outside the responsibility of the job holder are referred to an authorised person	Speak to communicate information, ideas and opinions adapting speech and content to take account of the listener(s) and medium.	Speaking and Listening Level 1		
3.7 work is carried out to approved procedures and practices and in compliance with statutory requirements	Read and obtain information of varying length and detail from different sources.	Reading Level 2		

Unit PRO2: Contribute to health and safety in the workplace

Element 1: Operate safely in the workplace

National Standard of Work	Literacy National Standard	Level Title	Numeracy National Standard	Level Title
1.1 work activities are carried out safely to avoid creating hazardous situations that may endanger operators of the work and other personnel	Read and obtain information of varying length and detail from different sources.	Reading Level 2		
1.2 hazards and potential hazards identified in the workplace are dealt with appropriately within the responsibility and capability of the work operator and reported promptly to the appropriate person(s)	Speak to communicate information, ideas and opinions adapting speech and content to take account of the listener(s) and medium. Read and obtain information from different sources.	Speaking and Listening Level 1 Reading Level 1		
1.3 communications are clear and information or instruction is confirmed as understood	Speak to communicate information, ideas and opinions adapting speech and content to take account of the listener(s) and medium.	Speaking and Listening Level 1		
1.4 all tools and equipment are used safely in accordance with organisational procedures, manufacturer's instructions and relevant statutory regulations	Read and obtain information of varying length and detail from different sources.	Reading Level 2		
1.5 work materials and components are handled and stored in accordance with approved procedures and practices	Read and obtain information from different sources.	Reading Level 1		
1.6 manual handling is carried out safely using appropriate handling techniques	Read and obtain information from different sources.	Reading Level 1		

Unit PR02: Contribute to health and safety in the workplace

Element 1: Operate safely in the workplace *(continued)*

National Standard of Work	Literacy National Standard	Level Title	Numeracy National Standard	Level Title
1.7 accident(s) and incident(s) are reported promptly to an authorised person in accordance with approved procedures and practices	Speak to communicate information, ideas and opinions adapting speech and content to take account of the listener(s) and medium. Read and obtain information of varying length and detail from different sources.	Speaking and Listening Level 1 Reading Level 2		
1.8 appropriate personal protective equipment is used in compliance with safe working practices	Read and obtain information from different sources.	Reading Level 1		
1.9 work is carried out to approved procedures and practices and in compliance with statutory requirements	Read and obtain information of varying length and detail from different sources.	Reading Level 2		

Getting the basics right in Construction (Plant and Accessing)

Unit PRO2: Contribute to health and safety in the workplace

Element 2: Respond to emergencies

National Standard of Work	Literacy National Standard	Level Title	Numeracy National Standard	Level Title
2.1 in the event of an emergency, procedures are implemented promptly and correctly in accordance with recognised safe practice and organisational policy	Read and obtain information of varying length and detail from different sources.	Reading Level 2		
2.2 accident(s) and incident(s) are responded to within the responsibility and capability of the work operator and promptly reported to an authorised person	Read and obtain information from different sources. Speak to communicate information, ideas and opinions adapting speech and content to take account of the listener(s) and medium.	Reading Level 1 Speaking and Listening Level 1		
2.3 use of emergency appliances is carried out in accordance with approved procedures and practices	Read and obtain information from different sources.	Reading Level 1		
2.4 details of accident(s) and incident(s) are recorded in accordance with approved procedures and practices	Write to communicate information, ideas and opinions clearly using length, format and style appropriate to purpose and audience.	Writing Level 1		
2.5 problems and conditions outside the responsibility of the job holder are referred to an authorised person	Speak to communicate information, ideas and opinions adapting speech and content to take account of the listener(s) and medium.	Speaking and Listening Level 1		

Unit PR02: Contribute to health and safety in the workplace

Element 3: Assist in the security of the workplace

National Standard of Work	Literacy National Standard	Level Title	Numeracy National Standard	Level Title
3.1 unauthorised personnel seen in the workplace are dealt with in accordance with organisational procedures and the appropriate person(s) advised	Read and obtain information from different sources. Speak to communicate information, ideas and opinions adapting speech and content to take account of the listener(s) and medium.	Reading Level 1 Speaking and Listening Level 1		
3.2 arrangements for security are observed and maintained in accordance with approved procedures and practices	Read and obtain information from different sources.	Reading Level 1		
3.3 potential risks to security are reported promptly to the appropriate person(s) and remedial action taken as necessary in accordance with organisational procedures	Speak to communicate information, ideas and opinions adapting speech and content to take account of the listener(s) and medium. Read and obtain information from different sources.	Speaking and Listening Level 2 Reading Level 1		
3.4 breaches of security are reported immediately to an authorised person				
3.5 problems and conditions outside the responsibility of the job holder are referred to an authorised person	Speak to communicate information, ideas and opinions adapting speech and content to take account of the listener(s) and medium.	Speaking and Listening Level 1		

Unit PR13: Assist in the efficiency of the workplace

Element 1: Maintain a clean and tidy work station

National Standard of Work	Literacy National Standard	Level Title	Numeracy National Standard	Level Title
1.1 the work station is maintained clean and tidy so that it complements the work activity and the surrounding environment	N/A			
1.2 waste and debris are disposed of in designated receptacles or locations in accordance with instruction and approved procedures and practices	Listen and respond to spoken language, including information and narratives, and follow explanations and instructions of varying length, adapting response to speaker, medium and context. Read and obtain information from different sources.	Speaking and Listening Level 1 Reading Level 1		
1.3 work tools and equipment not is use are stored and housed safely in the designated place	N/A			
1.4 work materials and components are stored in accordance with approved procedures and practices	Read and obtain information from different sources.	Reading Level 1		
1.5 harmful materials are removed or reported to an authorised person for further action	Speak to communicate information, ideas and opinions adapting speech and content to take account of the listener(s) and medium.	Speaking and Listening Level 1		
1.6 problems and conditions outside the responsibility of the job holder are referred to an authorised person				
1.7 work is carried out to approved procedures and practices and in compliance with statutory requirements	Read and obtain information of varying length and detail from different sources.	Reading Level 2		

Unit PR13: Assist in the efficiency of the workplace

Element 2: Maintain tools and equipment

National Standard of Work	Literacy National Standard	Level Title	Numeracy National Standard	Level Title
2.1 tools and equipment are maintained in a clean and usable condition	N/A			
2.2 powered equipment is shut down and isolated from the power source prior to any maintenance	N/A			
2.3 equipment is maintained in accordance with the manufacturers' recommendations	Read and obtain information of varying length and detail from different sources.	Reading Level 2		
2.4 tools and equipment are confirmed as operational and safe for use	Speak to communicate information, ideas and opinions adapting speech and content to take account of the listener(s) and medium.	Speaking and Listening Level 1		
2.5 damage to tools and equipment is reported to an authorised person				
2.6 problems and conditions outside the responsibility of the job holder are referred to an authorised person				
2.7 work is carried out to approved procedures and in compliance with statutory requirements	Read and obtain information of varying length and detail from different sources.	Reading Level 2		

Unit PR13: Assist in the efficiency of the workplace

Element 3: Organise your own work and maintain standards

National Standard of Work	Literacy National Standard	Level Title	Numeracy National Standard	Level Title
3.1 work is organised to comply with instructions and the agreed schedules	Listen and respond to spoken language, including information and narratives, and follow explanations and instructions of varying length, adapting response to speaker, medium and context. Read and obtain information from different sources.	Speaking and Listening Level 1 Reading Level 1	Read and understand information given by numbers, symbols, diagrams and charts used for different purposes and in different ways in graphical, numerical and written material.	Understanding and using mathematical information Entry 3
3.2 work methods are employed in accordance with approved procedures and practices and optimise the use of time	Read and obtain information from different sources.	Reading Level 1	Generate results to a given level of accuracy using given methods, measures and checking procedures appropriate to the specified purpose – use common measures.	Calculating and manipulating mathematical information Entry 3
3.3 your own work is co-ordinated with other relevant personnel and related activities as required	Engage in discussion with one or more people in familiar and unfamiliar situations, making clear and relevant contributions that respond to what others say and produce a shared understanding about different topics.	Speaking and Listening Level 1		
3.4 any suggestions for improvements to work methods are referred to an authorised person for confirmation and agreement on the action to be taken	Speak to communicate straightforward and detailed information, ideas and opinions clearly, adapting speech and content to take account of the listener(s), medium, purpose and situation.	Speaking and Listening Level 2		
3.5 work is done to the agreed standards and is in accordance with the specification and the organisational policy	Read and obtain information from different sources.	Reading Level 1		
3.6 deviations in standard or specification are agreed with an authorised person	Speak to communicate information, ideas and opinions adapting speech and content to take account of the listener(s) and medium.	Speaking and Listening Level 1		

Unit PR13: Assist in the efficiency of the workplace

Element 3: Organise your own work and maintain standards *(continued)*

National Standard of Work	Literacy National Standard	Level Title	Numeracy National Standard	Level Title
3.7 work that may be detrimental to safety or the environment is referred to the appropriate person(s) in accordance with organisational and operational procedures	Speak to communicate information, ideas and opinions adapting speech and content to take account of the listener(s) and medium. Read and obtain information from different sources.	Speaking and Listening Level 1 Reading Level 1		
3.8 waste and debris are removed and disposed of in accordance with approved procedures and practices	Read and obtain information from different sources.	Reading Level 1		
3.9 work is carried out to approved procedures and practices and in compliance with statutory requirements	Read and obtain information of varying length and detail from different sources.	Reading Level 2		

Unit PR 14: Operate powered tools and equipment for routine and predictable requirements

Element 1: Prepare powered tools and equipment for use

National Standard of Work	Literacy National Standard	Level Title	Numeracy National Standard	Level Title
1.1 operations requiring the use of powered tools and equipment are identified and confirmed in accordance with the specifications and work instructions	Read and obtain information from different sources. Listen and respond to spoken language, including information and narratives, and follow explanations and instructions of varying length, adapting response to speaker, medium and context.	Reading Level 1 Speaking and Listening Level 1		
1.2 pre-start inspections are carried out on the powered tools and equipment in accordance with approved procedures and practices	Read and obtain information from different sources.	Reading Level 1		
1.3 any defect(s) of the powered tools and equipment are identified, recorded and appropriate action taken to correct them	Speak to communicate information, ideas and opinions adapting speech and content to take account of the listener(s) and medium. Write to communicate information, ideas and opinions clearly using length, format and style appropriate to purpose and audience.	Speaking and Listening Level 1 Writing Level 1		
1.4 powered tools and equipment are confirmed safe, correct and ready for use in accordance with the work requirements and approved procedures and practices	Speak to communicate information, ideas and opinions adapting speech and content to take account of the listener(s) and medium. Read and obtain information from different sources.	Speaking and Listening Level 1 Reading Level 1		
1.5 problems and conditions outside the responsibility of the candidate are referred to an authorised person	Speak to communicate information, ideas and opinions adapting speech and content to take account of the listener(s) and medium.	Speaking and Listening Level 1		
1.6 work is carried out to approved procedures and practices and in compliance with statutory requirements	Read and obtain information of varying length and detail from different sources.	Reading Level 2		

Unit PR 14: Operate powered tools and equipment for routine and predictable requirements

Element 2: Run and operate powered tools and equipment

National Standard of Work	Literacy National Standard	Level Title	Numeracy National Standard	Level Title
2.1 start and stop procedures are carried out to confirm functions are in accordance with safe control and the manufacturer's operating instructions	Read and obtain information of varying length and detail from different sources.	Reading Level 2		
2.2 powered tools and equipment are run and operated to the work requirement	Read and obtain information from different sources.	Reading Level 1		
2.3 operations are carried out safely in accordance with specifications and approved procedures and practices	Read and obtain information from different sources.	Reading Level 1		
2.4 defects in performance are identified, recorded and reported to the appropriate person(s)	Speak to communicate information, ideas and opinions adapting speech and content to take account of the listener(s) and medium. Write to communicate information, ideas and opinions clearly using length, format and style appropriate to purpose and audience.	Speaking and Listening Level 1 Writing Level 1		
2.5 problems and conditions outside the responsibility of the candidate are referred to an authorised person	Speak to communicate information, ideas and opinions adapting speech and content to take account of the listener(s) and medium.	Speaking and Listening Level 1		
2.6 work is carried out to approved procedures and practices and in compliance with statutory requirements	Read and obtain information of varying length and detail from different sources.	Reading Level 2		

Getting the basics right in Construction (Plant and Accessing)

Unit PR 14: Operate powered tools and equipment for routine and predictable requirements

Element 3: Shut down and carry out post-stop checks on powered tools and equipment

National Standard of Work	Literacy National Standard	Level Title	Numeracy National Standard	Level Title
3.1 powered tools and equipment are stopped safely in accordance with approved procedures and practices	Read and obtain information from different sources.	Reading Level 1		
3.2 post-stop checks are carried out in accordance with organisational and operational procedure	Read and obtain information from different sources.	Reading Level 1		
3.3 defects and replacement needs are identified, recorded and reported to the appropriate person(s)	Speak to communicate information, ideas and opinions adapting speech and content to take account of the listener(s) and medium. Write to communicate information, ideas and opinions clearly using length, format and style appropriate to purpose and audience.	Speaking and Listening Level 1 Writing Level 1		
3.4 powered tools and equipment are confirmed safe, correct and ready for use in accordance with the work requirements and approved procedures and practices	Read and obtain information from different sources.	Reading Level 1		
3.5 problems and conditions outside the responsibility of the candidate are referred to an authorised person	Speak to communicate information, ideas and opinions adapting speech and content to take account of the listener(s) and medium.	Speaking and Listening Level 1		
3.6 work is carried out to approved procedures and practices and in compliance with statutory requirements	Read and obtain information of varying length and detail from different sources.	Reading Level 2		

Unit PR15: Assist with the specified work activity

Element 1: Receive information and instruction to assist the work activity

National Standard of Work	Literacy National Standard	Level Title	Numeracy National Standard	Level Title
1.1 receive and confirm the understanding of information and instruction for the work activity	Listen and respond to spoken language, including information and narratives, and follow explanations and instructions of varying length, adapting response to speaker, medium and context. Read and obtain information from different sources.	Speaking and Listening Level 1 Reading Level 1		
1.2 circumstances of the work activity and its environment that differ from and are not compatible with the information and instruction are reported and referred to an authorised person	Speak to communicate information, ideas and opinions adapting speech and content to take account of the listener(s) and medium. Read and obtain information from different sources.	Speaking and Listening Level 1 Reading Level 1		
1.3 amendment and changes to information and instruction are confirmed and agreed with the appropriate person(s) in accordance with approved procedures and practices	Speak to communicate information, ideas and opinions adapting speech and content to take account of the listener(s) and medium. Read and obtain information from different sources.	Speaking and Listening Level 1 Reading Level 1		
1.4 where information is unclear, safety is not compromised and further clarification of information and instruction is sought	Engage in discussion with one or more people in familiar and unfamiliar situations, making clear and relevant contributions that respond to what others say and produce a shared understanding about different topics.	Speaking and Listening Level 1		
1.5 work is carried out to approved procedures and practices and in compliance with statutory requirements	Read and obtain information of varying length and detail from different sources.	Reading Level 2		

Unit PR15: Assist with the specified work activity

Element 2: Move and store materials and components to assist the work activity

National Standard of Work	Literacy National Standard	Level Title	Numeracy National Standard	Level Title
2.1 moving and storing of materials and components is carried out safely to instruction and the work requirements	Listen and respond to spoken language, including information and narratives, and follow explanations and instructions of varying length, adapting response to speaker, medium and context. Read and obtain information from different sources.	Speaking and Listening Level 1 Reading Level 1		
2.2 hazardous materials and components are identified, made safe or removed in accordance with approved procedures and practices	Read and obtain information from different sources.	Reading Level 1		
2.3 movement of materials and components is carried out without endangering the work operator or others in accordance with approved procedures and practices	Read and obtain information from different sources.	Reading Level 1		
2.4 waste and harmful materials are disposed of in a manner that minimises danger to the environment in accordance with approved procedures and practices	Read and obtain information from different sources.	Reading Level 1		
2.5 the work area is tidily maintained in accordance with customer and organisational requirements	Read and obtain information from different sources.	Reading Level 1		
2.6 problems and conditions outside the responsibility of the candidate are referred to the authorised person	Speak to communicate information, ideas and opinions adapting speech and content to take account of the listener(s) and medium.	Speaking and Listening Level 1		

Unit PR15: Assist with the specified work activity

Element 2: Move and store materials and components to assist the work activity *(continued)*

National Standard of Work	Literacy National Standard	Level Title	Numeracy National Standard	Level Title
2.7 work is carried out to approved procedures and practices and in compliance with statutory requirements	Read and obtain information of varying length and detail from different sources.	Reading Level 2		

Unit PR15: Assist with the specified work activity

Element 3: Assist the work activity to requirements

National Standard of Work	Literacy National Standard	Level Title	Numeracy National Standard	Level Title
3.1 assistance with the work activity is carried out to instruction and in accordance with requirements	Listen and respond to spoken language, including information and narratives, and follow explanations and instructions of varying length, adapting response to speaker, medium and context.	Speaking and Listening Level 1	Generate results to a given level of accuracy using methods, measures and checking procedures appropriate to the specified purpose – use whole numbers – use common measures.	Calculating and manipulating mathematical information Level 1
3.2 work done is to the required standards and specification of the work requirement	Read and obtain information from different sources.	Reading Level 1		
3.3 tools and equipment used with the work activity are safe and in accordance with the approved procedures and practices	Read and obtain information from different sources.	Reading Level 1		
3.4 work is carried out in a manner to help minimise damage and disruption to the surrounding environment	N/A			
3.5 problems and conditions outside the responsibility of the candidate are referred to the authorised person	Speak to communicate information, ideas and opinions adapting speech and content to take account of the listener(s) and medium.	Speaking and Listening Level 1		
3.6 work is carried out to approved procedures and practices and in compliance with statutory requirements	Read and obtain information of varying length and detail from different sources.	Reading Level 2		

Unit CR01: Set up protection and safety equipment for the working area (basic)

Element 1: Install and maintain protection and safety equipment for the working area

National Standard of Work	Literacy National Standard	Level Title	Numeracy National Standard	Level Title
1.1 area for the intended work activity is identified in accordance with the instructions and operational requirements	Listen and respond to spoken language, including information and narratives, and follow explanations and instructions of varying length, adapting response to speaker, medium and context. Read and obtain information from different sources.	Speaking and Listening Level 1 Reading Level 1		
1.2 protection and safety equipment which meets the operational requirements is obtained and made ready for use	Read and obtain information from different sources.	Reading Level 1		
1.3 the protection and safety equipment is handled and positioned correctly in accordance with instruction and the work requirements	Listen and respond to spoken language, including information and narratives, and follow explanations and instructions of varying length, adapting response to speaker, medium and context. Read and obtain information from different sources.	Speaking and Listening Level 1 Reading Level 1		
1.4 any special arrangements are confirmed and provided for in accordance with instruction and specifications	Listen and respond to spoken language, including information and narratives, and follow explanations and instructions of varying length, adapting response to speaker, medium and context. Read and obtain information from different sources.	Speaking and Listening Level 1 Reading Level 1		
1.5 the integrity of the protection and safety equipment is maintained in accordance with instruction and progress of the work activity	Read and obtain information from different sources. Listen and respond to spoken language, including information and narratives, and follow explanations and instructions of varying length, adapting response to speaker, medium and context.	Reading Level 1 Speaking and Listening Level 1		

National Standard of Work	Literacy National Standard	Level Title	Numeracy National Standard	Level Title
1.6 problems and conditions outside the responsibility of the job holder are referred to an appropriate person	Speak to communicate information, ideas and opinions adapting speech and content to take account of the listener(s) and medium.	Speaking and Listening Level 1		
1.7 work is carried out to approved procedures and practices and in compliance with statutory requirements	Read and obtain information of varying length and detail from different sources.	Reading Level 2		

Unit CR01: Set up protection and safety equipment for the working area (basic)

Element 2: Remove protection and safety equipment from the working area

National Standard of Work	Literacy National Standard	Level Title	Numeracy National Standard	Level Title
2.1 removal of protection and safety equipment is safely carried out in accordance with instructions and approved procedures and practices	Listen and respond to spoken language, including information and narratives, and follow explanations and instructions of varying length, adapting response to speaker, medium and context. Read and obtain information from different sources.	Speaking and Listening Level 1 Reading Level 1		
2.2 all protection and safety equipment is accurately accounted for and shortfalls reported to the appropriate person	Speak to communicate information, ideas and opinions adapting speech and content to take account of the listener(s) and medium.	Speaking and Listening Level 1	Generate results to a given level of accuracy using methods, measures and checking procedures appropriate to the specified purpose – use whole numbers.	Calculating and manipulating mathematical information Level 1
2.3 the protection and safety equipment is returned to correct storage location and made available for re-use	N/A			
2.4 defective and damaged protection and safety equipment is reported to an authorised person for appropriate action	Speak to communicate information, ideas and opinions adapting speech and content to take account of the listener(s) and medium.	Speaking and Listening Level 1		
2.5 problems and conditions outside the responsibility of the job holder are referred to an appropriate person	Speak to communicate information, ideas and opinions adapting speech and content to take account of the listener(s) and medium.	Speaking and Listening Level 1		
2.6 work is carried out to approved procedures and practices and in compliance with statutory requirements	Read and obtain information of varying length and detail from different sources.	Reading Level 2		

Getting the basics right in Construction (Plant and Accessing)

Unit PR 07: Carry out slinging and signalling for the movement of loads

Element 1: Prepare and sling loads for lifting

National Standard of Work	Literacy National Standard	Level Title	Numeracy National Standard	Level Title
1.1 loads being moved are accurately identified from relevant information and instruction	Listen and respond to spoken language, including information and narratives, and follow explanations and instructions of varying length, adapting response to speaker, medium and context.	Speaking and Listening Level 1		
	Read and obtain information from different sources.	Reading Level 2		
1.2 slinging technique is chosen in accordance with the characteristics of the loads, the intended lift and approved procedures and practices	Read and obtain information from different sources.	Reading Level 1		
1.3 difficulties in carrying out the slinging and movement of loads are identified and clarified with the appropriate person(s)	Speak to communicate information, ideas and opinions adapting speech and content to take account of the listener(s) and medium.	Speaking and Listening Level 1		
1.4 slinging equipment is selected and confirmed suitable for load(s) to be lifted				
1.5 defects and faults relating to the slinging equipment are reported to the authorised person				
1.6 loads are prepared and slung in accordance with the chosen slinging technique	Read and obtain information from different sources.	Reading Level 1		
1.7 support and balance of the slung load is confirmed satisfactory and secure prior to movement	Speak to communicate information, ideas and opinions adapting speech and content to take account of the listener(s) and medium.	Speaking and Listening Level 1		
1.8 work is carried out to approved procedures and practices and in compliance with statutory requirements	Read and obtain information of varying length and detail from different sources.	Reading Level 2		

Unit PR 07: Carry out slinging and signalling for the movement of loads

Element 2: Direct and control the movement and placing of loads

National Standard of Work	Literacy National Standard	Level Title	Numeracy National Standard	Level Title
2.1 load movement and operations procedure are agreed with relevant personnel	Read and obtain information from different sources. Speak to communicate information, ideas and opinions adapting speech and content to take account of the listener(s) and medium.	Reading Level 1 Speaking and Listening Level 1		
2.2 method of signalling and communication is confirmed and established with relevant personnel prior to the commencement of any movement operations	Speak to communicate information, ideas and opinions adapting speech and content to take account of the listener(s) and medium.	Speaking and Listening Level 1		
2.3 signalling and communication are carried out in accordance with approved procedures and practices	Read and obtain information from different sources.	Reading Level 1		
2.4 movement of load is directed to its destination accurately using agreed signalling code	N/A			
2.5 unclear signalling and communication are responded to promptly and clarified so as not to endanger personnel or operations	Speak to communicate information, ideas and opinions adapting speech and content to take account of the listener(s) and medium.	Speaking and Listening Level 1		
2.6 stability of load is monitored throughout movement and on release of load	N/A			
2.7 load is positioned, set down and the sling relaxed for the removal of the lifting equipment	N/A			
2.8 work is carried out to approved procedures and practices and in compliance with statutory requirements	Read and obtain information of varying length and detail from different sources.	Reading Level 2		

7. Progression from the Adult Literacy Standards to the Adult Literacy Core Curriculum

National Standards for Adult Literacy

The progression between capabilities

Entry Level		

ENTRY 1 LEVEL	**ENTRY 2 LEVEL**	**ENTRY 3 LEVEL**
Speaking and listening *At this level, adults can*	***Speaking and listening*** *At this level, adults can*	***Speaking and listening*** *At this level, adults can*
listen and respond to spoken language, including simple narratives, statements, questions and single-step instructions	**listen and respond** to spoken language, including straightforward information, short narratives, explanations and instructions	**listen and respond** to spoken language, including straightforward information and narratives, and follow straightforward explanations and instructions, both face to face and on the telephone
speak to communicate basic information, feelings and opinions on familiar topics	**speak to communicate** information, feelings and opinions on familiar topics	**speak to communicate** information, feelings and opinions on familiar topics, using appropriate formality, both face to face and on the telephone
engage in discussion with another person in a familiar situation about familiar topics	**engage in discussion** with one or more people in a familiar situation to establish shared understanding about familiar topics	**engage in discussion** with one or more people in a familiar situation, making relevant points and responding to what others say to reach a shared understanding about familiar topics
Reading *At this level, adults can*	***Reading*** *At this level, adults can*	***Reading*** *At this level, adults can*
read and understand short texts with repeated language patterns on familiar topics	**read and understand** short, straightforward texts on familiar topics	**read and understand** short, straightforward texts on familiar topics accurately and independently
read and obtain information from common signs and symbols	**read and obtain information** from short documents, familiar sources and signs and symbols	**read and obtain information** from everyday sources
Writing *At this level, adults can*	***Writing*** *At this level, adults can*	***Writing*** *At this level, adults can*
write to communicate information to an intended audience	**write to communicate** information with some awareness of the intended audience	**write to communicate** information and opinions with some adaptation to the intended audience

LEVEL 1	LEVEL 2
Speaking and listening *At this level, adults can*	**Speaking and listening** *At this level, adults can*
listen and respond to spoken language, including information and narratives, and follow explanations and instructions of varying lengths, adapting response to speaker, medium and context	**listen and respond** to spoken language, including extended information and narratives, and follow detailed explanations and multi-step instructions of varying length, adapting response to speaker, medium and context
speak to communicate information, ideas and opinions adapting speech and content to take account of the listener(s) and medium	**speak to communicate** straightforward and detailed information, ideas and opinions clearly, adapting speech and content to take account of the listener(s), medium, purpose and situation
engage in discussion with one or more people in familiar and unfamiliar situations, making clear and relevant contributions that respond to what others say and produce a shared understanding about different topics	**engage in discussion** with one or more people in a variety of different situations, making clear and effective contributions that produce outcomes appropriate to purpose and topic
Reading *At this level, adults can*	**Reading** *At this level, adults can*
read and understand straightforward texts of varying length on a variety of topics accurately and independently	**read and understand** a range of texts of varying complexity accurately and independently
read and obtain information from different sources	**read and obtain information** of varying length and detail from different sources
Writing *At this level, adults can*	**Writing** *At this level, adults can*
write to communicate information, ideas and opinions clearly using length, format and style appropriate to purpose and audience	**write to communicate** information, ideas and opinions clearly and effectively, using length, format and style appropriate to purpose, content and audience

Speaking and listening: the progression between curriculum elements

<table>
<tr><td colspan="4" align="center">Entry Level</td></tr>
<tr>
<th>TEXT FOCUS</th>
<th>ENTRY 1 LEVEL</th>
<th>ENTRY 2 LEVEL</th>
</tr>
<tr>
<td>Listen and respond</td>
<td>
SLlr/E1.1 Listen for the gist of short explanations

SLlr/E1.2 Listen for detail using key words to extract some specific information

SLlr/E1.3 Follow single-step instructions in a familiar context, asking for instructions to be repeated if necessary

SLlr/E1.4 Listen and respond to requests for personal information
</td>
<td>
SLlr/E2.1 Listen for and follow the gist of explanations, instructions and narratives

SLlr/E2.2 Listen for detail in short explanations, instructions and narratives

SLlr/E2.3 Listen for and identify the main points of short explanations or presentations

SLlr/E2.4 Listen to and follow short, straightforward explanations and instructions

SLlr/E2.5 Listen to and identify simply expressed feelings and opinions

SLlr/E2.6 Respond to straightforward questions
</td>
</tr>
<tr>
<td>Speak to communicate</td>
<td>
SLc/E1.1 Speak clearly to be heard and understood in simple exchanges

SLc/E1.2 Make requests using appropriate terms

SLc/E1.3 Ask questions to obtain specific information

SLc/E1.4 Make statements of fact clearly
</td>
<td>
SLc/E2.1 Speak clearly to be heard and understood in straightforward exchanges

SLc/E2.2 Make requests and ask questions to obtain information in everyday contexts

SLc/E2.3 Express clearly statements of fact, and short accounts and descriptions

SLc/E2.4 Ask questions to clarify understanding
</td>
</tr>
<tr>
<td>Engage in discussion</td>
<td>
SLd/E1.1 Speak and listen in simple exchanges and everyday contexts
</td>
<td>
SLd/E2.1 Follow the gist of discussions

SLd/E2.2 Follow the main points and make appropriate contributions to the discussion
</td>
</tr>
</table>

ENTRY LEVEL 3	LEVEL 1	LEVEL 2
SLlr/E3.1 Listen for and follow the gist of explanations, instructions and narratives in different contexts **SLlr/E3.2** Listen for detail in explanations, instructions and narratives in different contexts **SLlr/E3.3** Listen for and identify relevant information and new information from discussions, explanations and presentations **SLlr/E3.4** Use strategies to clarify and confirm understanding (e.g. facial expressions or gestures) **SLlr/E3.5** Listen to and respond appropriately to other points of view **SLlr/E3.6** Respond to a range of questions about familiar topics	**SLlr/L1.1** Listen for and identify relevant information from explanations and presentations on a range of straightforward topics **SLlr/L1.2** Listen for and understand explanations, instructions and narratives on different topics in a range of contexts **SLlr/L1.3** Use strategies to clarify and confirm understanding (e.g. facial expressions, body language and verbal prompts) **SLlr/L1.4** Provide feedback and confirmation when listening to others **SLlr/L1.5** Make contributions relevant to the situation and the subject **SLlr/L1.6** Respond to questions on a range of topics	**SLlr/L2.1** Listen for and identify relevant information from extended explanations or presentations on a range of topics **SLlr/L2.2** Listen to, understand and follow lengthy or multi-step instructions and narratives on a range of topics and in a range of contexts **SLlr/L2.3** Respond to detailed or extended questions on a range of topics **SLlr/L2.4** Respond to criticism and criticise constructively
SLc/E3.1 Speak clearly to be heard and understood using appropriate clarity, speed and phrasing **SLc/E3.2** Use formal language and register when appropriate **SLc/E3.3** Express clearly statements of fact and give short explanations, accounts and descriptions **SLc/E3.4** Make requests and ask questions to obtain information in familiar and unfamiliar contexts	**SLc/L1.1** Speak clearly in a way which suits the situation **SLc/L1.2** Make requests and ask questions to obtain information in familiar and unfamiliar contexts **SLc/L1.3** Express clearly statements of fact, explanations, instructions, accounts, and descriptions **SLc/L1.4** Present information and ideas in a logical sequence and include detail and develop ideas where appropriate	**SLc/L2.1** Speak clearly and confidently in a way which suits the situation **SLc/L2.2** Make requests and ask questions to obtain detailed information in familiar and unfamiliar contexts **SLc/L2.3** Express clearly statements of fact, explanations, instructions, accounts, descriptions using appropriate structure, style and vocabulary **SLc/L2.4** Present information and ideas in a logical sequence and provide further detail and development to clarify or confirm understanding
SLd/E3.1 Follow and understand the main points of discussions on different topics **SLd/E3.2** Make contributions to discussions that are relevant to the subject **SLd/E3.3** Respect the turn-taking rights of others during discussions	**SLd/L1.1** Follow and contribute to discussions on a range of straightforward topics **SLd/L1.2** Respect the turn-taking rights of others during discussions **SLd/L1.3** Use appropriate phrases for interruption	**SLd/L2.1** Make relevant contributions and help to move discussions forward **SLd/L2.2** Adapt contributions to discussions to suit audience, context, purpose and situation **SLd/L2.3** Use appropriate phrases for interruption and change of topic **SLd/L2.4** Support opinions and arguments with evidence **SLd/L2.5** Use strategies intended to reassure (e.g. body language and appropriate phraseology)

Reading and Writing (Text focus): the progression between curriculum elements

READING ☐   WRITING ☐

Entry Level		

TEXT FOCUS	**ENTRY LEVEL 1**	**ENTRY LEVEL 2**
Reading comprehension	**Rt/E1.1** Follow a short narrative on a familiar topic or experience **Rt/E1.2** Recognise the different purposes of texts at this level	**Rt/E2.1** Trace and understand the main events of chronological and instructional texts **Rt/E2.2** Recognise the different purposes of texts at this level **Rt/E2.3** Identify common sources of information **Rt/E2.4** Use illustrations and captions to locate information
Writing composition	**Wt/E1.1** Use written words and phrases to record or present information	**Wt/E2.1** Use written words and phrases to record or present information

ENTRY LEVEL 3	LEVEL 1	LEVEL 2
Rt/E3.1 Trace and understand the main events of chronological, continuous descriptive and explanatory texts of more than one paragraph **Rt/E3.2** Recognise the different purposes of texts at this level **Rt/E3.3** Recognise and understand the organisational features and typical language of instructional texts (e.g. use of imperatives and second person) **Rt/E3.4** Identify the main points and ideas, and predict words from context **Rt/E3.5** Understand and use organisational features to locate information (e.g. contents, index, menus) **Rt/E3.6** Skim read title, headings and illustrations to decide if material is of interest **Rt/E3.7** Scan texts to locate information **Rt/E3.8** Obtain specific information through detailed reading **Rt/E3.9** Relate an image to print and use it to obtain meaning	**Rt/L1.1** Trace and understand the main events of continuous descriptive, explanatory and persuasive texts **Rt/L1.2** Recognise how language and other textual features are used to achieve different purposes (e.g. to instruct, explain, describe, persuade) **Rt/L1.3** Identify the main points and specific detail, and infer meaning from images which is not explicit in the text **Rt/L1.4** Use organisational and structural features to locate information (e.g. contents, index, menus, subheadings, paragraphs) **Rt/L1.5** Use different reading strategies to find and obtain information	**Rt/L2.1** Trace and understand the main events of continuous descriptive, explanatory and persuasive texts **Rt/L2.2** Identify the purpose of a text and infer meaning which is not explicit **Rt/L2.3** Identify the main points and specific detail **Rt/L2.4** Read an argument and identify the points of view **Rt/L2.5** Read critically to evaluate information, and compare information, ideas and opinions from different sources **Rt/L2.6** Use organisational features and systems to locate texts and information **Rt/L2.7** Use different reading strategies to find and obtain information (e.g. skimming, scanning, detailed reading) **Rt/L2.8** Summarise information from longer documents
Wt/E3.1 Plan and draft writing **Wt/E3.2** Organise writing in short paragraphs **Wt/E3.3** Sequence chronological writing **Wt/E3.4** Proof-read and correct writing for grammar and spelling	**Wt/L1.1** Plan and draft writing **Wt/L1.2** Judge how much to write and the level of detail to include **Wt/L1.3** Present information in a logical sequence using paragraphs where appropriate **Wt/L1.4** Use language suitable for purpose and audience **Wt/L1.5** Use format and structure for different purposes **Wt/L1.6** Proof-read and revise writing for accuracy and meaning	**Wt/L2.1** Plan and draft writing **Wt/L2.2** Judge how much to write and the level of detail to include **Wt/L2.3** Present information and ideas in a logical or persuasive sequence, using paragraphs where appropriate **Wt/L2.4** Use format and structure to organise writing for different purposes **Wt/L2.5** Use formal and informal language appropriate to purpose and audience **Wt/L2.6** Use different styles of writing for different purposes (e.g. persuasive techniques, supporting evidence, technical vocabulary) **Wt/L2.7** Proof-read and revise writing for accuracy and meaning

Reading and Writing (Sentence focus): the progression between curriculum elements

READING ☐   WRITING ▨

Entry Level		

TEXT FOCUS	**ENTRY LEVEL 1**	**ENTRY LEVEL 2**
Grammar and punctuation	**Rs/E1.1** Read and recognise simple sentence structures	**Rs/E2.1** Read and understand linking words and adverbials in instructions and directions (e.g. *next, then, right* and *straight on*) **Rs/E2.2** Use knowledge of simple sentence structure and word order to help decipher unfamiliar words and predict meaning **Rs/E2.3** Apply own life experience and knowledge to check out plausible meanings of a sentence as a whole when decoding unfamiliar words **Rs/E2.4** Use punctuation and capitalisation to aid understanding
Grammar and punctuation	**Ws/E1.1** Construct a simple sentence **Ws/E1.2** Punctuate a simple sentence with a capital letter and a full stop **Ws/E1.3** Use a capital letter for personal pronoun 'I'	**Ws/E2.1** Construct simple and compound sentences, using common conjunctions to connect two clauses (e.g. *as, and, but*) **Ws/E2.2** Use adjectives **Ws/E2.3** Use punctuation correctly (e.g. capital letters, full stops and question marks) **Ws/E2.4** Use a capital letter for proper nouns

Rs/E3.1 Recognise and understand the organisational features and typical language of instructional texts (e.g. use of imperatives, second person) **Rs/E3.2** Use implicit and explicit knowledge of different types of word (e.g. linking words [connectives], nouns, verbs, adjectives), of word order, and of possible plausible meanings, to help decode unfamiliar words and predict meaning **Rs/E3.3** Use punctuation and capitalisation to aid understanding	**Rs/L1.1** Use implicit and explicit grammatical knowledge (e.g. of different sentence forms, types of word, verb tense, word order) along with own knowledge and experience to predict meaning, try out plausible meanings, and to read and check for sense **Rs/L1.2** Use punctuation to help their understanding	**Rs/L2.1** Use implicit and explicit grammatical knowledge, alongside own knowledge and experience of context, to help follow meaning and judge the purpose of different types of text **Rs/L2.2** Use punctuation to help interpret the meaning and purpose of texts
Ws/E3.1 Write in complete sentences **Ws/E3.2** Use correct basic grammar (e.g. appropriate verb tense, subject–verb agreement) **Ws/E3.3** Use punctuation correctly (e.g. capital letters, full stops, question marks, exclamation marks)	**Ws/L1.1** Write in complete sentences **Ws/L1.2** Use correct grammar (e.g. subject–verb agreement, correct use of tense) **Ws/L1.3** Punctuate sentences correctly, and use punctuation so that meaning is clear	**Ws/L2.1** Construct complex sentences **Ws/L2.2** Use correct grammar (e.g. subject – verb agreement, correct and consistent use of tense) **Ws/L2.3** Use pronouns so that their meaning is clear **Ws/L2.4** Punctuate sentences correctly, and use punctuation accurately (e.g. commas, apostrophes, inverted commas)

Reading and Writing (Word focus): the progression between curriculum elements

READING ☐   WRITING ▦

Entry Level		
TEXT FOCUS	**ENTRY LEVEL 1**	**ENTRY LEVEL 2**
Vocabulary, word recognition and phonics	**Rw/E1.1** Possess a limited, meaningful sight vocabulary of words, signs and symbols **Rw/E1.2** Decode simple, regular words **Rw/E1.3** Recognise the letters of the alphabet in both upper and lower case	**Rw/E2.1** Read and understand words on forms related to personal information (e.g. first name, surname, address, postcode, age, date of birth) **Rw/E2.2** Recognise high-frequency words and words with common spelling patterns **Rw/E2.3** Use phonic and graphic knowledge to decode words **Rw/E2.4** Use a simplified dictionary to find the meaning of unfamiliar words **Rw/E2.5** Use initial letters to find and sequence words in alphabetical order
Spelling and handwriting	**Ww/E1.1** Spell correctly some personal key words and familiar words **Ww/E1.2** Write the letters of the alphabet using upper and lower case **Ww/E1.3** Use basic sound–symbol association to help spelling, *as appropriate for the needs of the learner*	**Ww/E2.1** Spell correctly the majority of personal details and familiar common words **Ww/E2.2** Use their knowledge of sound–symbol relationships and phonological patterns (e.g. consonant clusters and vowel phonemes) to help work out correct spellings, *as appropriate for the needs of the learner* **Ww/E2.3** Produce legible text

ENTRY 3 LEVEL	LEVEL 1 LEVEL	LEVEL 2 LEVEL
Rw/E3.1 Recognise and understand relevant specialist key words **Rw/E3.2** Read and understand words and phrases commonly used on forms **Rw/E3.3** Use a dictionary to find the meaning of unfamiliar words **Rw/E3.4** Use first- and second-place letters to find and sequence words in alphabetical order **Rw/E3.5** Use a variety of reading strategies to help decode an increasing range of unfamiliar words	**Rw/L1.1** Use reference material to find the meaning of unfamiliar words **Rw/L1.2** Recognise and understand the vocabulary associated with different types of text, using appropriate strategies to work out meaning **Rw/L1.3** Recognise and understand an increasing range of vocabulary, applying knowledge of word structure, related words, word roots, derivations, borrowings	**Rw/L2.1** Read and understand technical vocabulary **Rw/L2.2** Use reference material to find the meaning of unfamiliar words **Rw/L2.3** Recognise and understand vocabulary associated with texts of different levels of accessibility, formality, complexity and of different purpose
Ww/E3.1 Spell correctly common words and relevant key words for work and special interest **Ww/E3.2** Use their developing knowledge of sound–symbol relationships and phonological patterns to help spell a greater range of words and longer words, *as appropriate for the needs of the learner* **Ww/E3.3** Produce legible text	**Ww/L1.1** Spell correctly words used most often in work, studies and daily life **Ww/L1.2** Produce legible text	**Ww/L2.1** Spell correctly words used most often in work, studies and daily life, including familiar technical words **Ww/L2.2** Produce legible text

8. Progression from the Adult Numeracy Standards to the Adult Numeracy Core Curriculum

National Standards for Adult Numeracy

The progression between capabilities

Entry Level		

ENTRY 1 LEVEL	ENTRY 2 LEVEL	ENTRY 3 LEVEL
Understanding and using mathematical information *At this level, adults can*	***Understanding and using mathematical information*** *At this level, adults can*	***Understanding and using mathematical information*** *At this level, adults can*
read and understand information given by numbers and symbols in simple graphical, numerical and written material	**read and understand** information given by numbers, symbols, simple diagrams and charts in graphical, numerical and written material	**read and understand** information given by numbers, symbols, diagrams and charts used for different purposes and in different ways in graphical, numerical and written material
specify and describe a practical problem or task using numbers and measures	**specify and describe** a practical problem or task using numbers, measures and simple shapes to record essential information	**specify and describe** a practical problem or task using numbers, measures and diagrams to collect and record relevant information
Calculating and manipulating mathematical information *At this level, adults can*	**Calculating and manipulating mathematical information** *At this level, adults can*	**Calculating and manipulating mathematical information** *At this level, adults can*
generate results which make sense and use given methods and given checking procedures appropriate to the specified purpose	**generate results** to a given level of accuracy using given methods and given checking procedures appropriate to the specified purpose	**generate results** to a given level of accuracy using given methods, measures and checking procedures appropriate to the specified purpose
Interpreting results and communicating mathematical information *At this level, adults can*	***Interpreting results and communicating mathematical information*** *At this level, adults can*	***Interpreting results and communicating mathematical information*** *At this level, adults can*
present and explain results which show an understanding of the intended purpose using appropriate numbers, measures, objects or pictures	**present and explain results** which meet the intended purpose using appropriate numbers, simple diagrams and symbols	**present and explain results** which meet the intended purpose using appropriate numbers, diagrams, charts and symbols

LEVEL 1	LEVEL 2
Understanding and using mathematical information *At this level, adults can*	*Understanding and using mathematical information* *At this level, adults can*
read and understand straightforward mathematical information used for different purposes and independently select relevant information from given graphical, numerical and written material	**read and understand** mathematical information used for different purposes and independently select and compare relevant information from a variety of graphical, numerical and written material
specify and describe a practical activity, problem or task using mathematical information and language to make accurate observations and identify suitable calculations to achieve an appropriate outcome	**specify and describe** a practical activity, problem or task using mathematical information and language to increase understanding and select appropriate methods for carrying through a substantial activity
Calculating and manipulating mathematical information *At this level, adults can*	**Calculating and manipulating mathematical information** *At this level, adults can*
generate results to a given level of accuracy using methods, measures and checking procedures appropriate to the specified purpose	**generate results** to an appropriate level of accuracy using methods, measures and checking procedures appropriate to the specified purpose
Interpreting results and communicating mathematical information *At this level, adults can*	*Interpreting results and communicating mathematical information* *At this level, adults can*
present and explain results which meet the intended purpose using an appropriate format to a given level of accuracy	**present and explain results** clearly and accurately using numerical, graphical and written formats appropriate to purpose, findings and audience

Number: the progression between curriculum elements

	Entry Level	
	ENTRY LEVEL 1	**ENTRY LEVEL 2**
Whole numbers	**N1/E1.1** Count reliably up to 10 items	**N1/E2.1** Count reliably up to 20 items
	N1/E1.2 Read and write numbers up to 10, including zero	**N1/E2.2** Read, write, order and compare numbers up to 100
	N1/E1.3 Order and compare numbers up to 10, including zero	**N1/E2.3** Add and subtract two-digit whole numbers
	N1/E1.4 Add single-digit numbers with totals to 10	**N1/E2.4** Recall addition and subtraction facts to 10
	N1/E1.5 Subtract single-digit numbers from numbers up to 10	**N1/E2.5** Multiply using single-digit whole numbers
	N1/E1.6 Interpret $+$, $-$ and $=$ in practical situations for solving problems	**N1/E2.6** Approximate by rounding to the nearest 10
	N1/E1.7 Use a calculator to check calculations using whole numbers	**N1/E2.7** Use and interpret $+$, $-$, $\times$ and $\div$ in practical situations for solving problems
		N1/E2.8 Use a calculator to check calculations using whole numbers
Fractions, decimals and percentages		**N2/E2.1** Read, write and compare halves and quarters of quantities
		N2/E2.2 Find halves and quarters of small numbers of items or shapes

Entry Level 3	Level 1	Level 2
N1/E3.1 Count, read, write, order and compare numbers up to 1000 **N1/E3.2** Add and subtract using three-digit whole numbers **N1/E3.3** Recall addition and subtraction facts to 20 **N1/E3.4** Multiply two-digit whole numbers by single-digit whole numbers **N1/E3.5** Recall multiplication facts (e.g. multiples of 2, 3, 4, 5, 10) **N1/E3.6** Divide two-digit whole numbers by single-digit whole numbers and interpret remainders **N1/E3.7** Approximate by rounding numbers less than 1000 to the nearest 10 or 100 **N1/E3.8** Estimate answers to calculations **N1/E3.9** Use and interpret $+$, $-$, $\times$, $\div$ and $=$ in practical situations for solving problems	**N1/L1.1** Read, write, order and compare numbers, including large numbers **N1/L1.2** Recognise negative numbers in practical contexts (e.g. temperatures) **N1/L1.3** Add, subtract, multiply and divide using efficient written methods **N1/L1.4** Multiply and divide whole numbers by 10 and 100 **N1/L1.5** Recall multiplication facts up to 10×10 and make connections with division facts **N1/L1.6** Recognise numerical relationships (e.g. multiples and squares) **N1/L1.7** Work out simple ratio and direct proportion **N1/L1.8** Approximate by rounding **N1/L1.9** Estimate answers to calculations	**N1/L2.1** Read, write, order and compare positive and negative numbers of any size in a practical context **N1/L2.2** Carry out calculations with numbers of any size using efficient methods **N1/L2.3** Calculate ratio and direct proportion **N1/L2.4** Evaluate expressions and make substitutions in given formulae in words and symbols to produce results
N2/E3.1 Read, write and understand common fractions (e.g. $\frac{3}{4}$, $\frac{2}{3}$, $\frac{1}{10}$) **N2/E3.2** Recognise and use equivalent forms (e.g. $\frac{5}{10} = \frac{1}{2}$) **N2/E3.3** Read, write and understand decimals up to two decimal places in practical contexts (such as: common measures to one decimal place, e.g. 1.5 m; money in decimal notation, e.g. £2.37) **N2/E3.4** Use a calculator to calculate using whole numbers and decimals to solve problems in context, and to check calculations	**N2/L1.1** Read, write, order and compare common fractions and mixed numbers **N2/L1.2** Find parts of whole number quantities or measurements (e.g. $\frac{2}{3}$ or $\frac{3}{4}$) **N2/L1.3** Recognise equivalencies between common fractions, percentages and decimals (e.g. 50% $= \frac{1}{2}$, 0.25 $= \frac{1}{4}$) and use these to find part of whole-number quantities **N2/L1.4** Read, write, order and compare decimals up to three decimal places **N2/L1.5** Add, subtract, multiply and divide decimals up to two places **N2/L1.6** Multiply and divide decimals by 10, 100 **N2/L1.7** Approximate decimals by rounding to a whole number or two decimal places **N2/L1.8** Read, write, order and compare simple percentages, and understand simple percentage increase and decrease **N2/L1.9** Find simple percentage parts of quantities and measurements **N2/L1.10** Find simple percentage increase and decrease **N2/L1.11** Use a calculator to calculate efficiently using whole numbers, fractions, decimals and percentages	**N2/L2.1** Use fractions to order and compare amounts or quantities **N2/L2.2** Identify equivalencies between fractions, decimals and percentages **N2/L2.3** Evaluate one number as a fraction of another **N2/L2.4** Use fractions to add and subtract amounts or quantities **N2/L2.5** Order, approximate and compare decimals when solving practical problems **N2/L2.6** Add, subtract, multiply and divide decimals up to three places **N2/L2.7** Order and compare percentages and understand percentage increase and decrease **N2/L2.8** Find percentage parts of quantities and measurements **N2/L2.9** Evaluate one number as a percentage of another **N2/L2.10** Use a calculator to calculate efficiently using whole numbers, fractions, decimals and percentages

Measures, shape and space: the progression between curriculum elements

	Entry Level	
	ENTRY LEVEL 1	**ENTRY LEVEL 2**
Common measures	**MSS1/E1.1** Recognise and select coins and notes **MSS1/E1.2** Relate familiar events to: times of the day; days of the week; seasons of the year **MSS1/E1.3** Describe size and use direct comparisons for the size of at least two items **MSS1/E1.4** Describe length, width, height, and use direct comparisons for length, width and height of items **MSS1/E1.5** Describe weight and use direct comparisons for the weight of items **MSS1/E1.6** Describe capacity and use direct comparisons for the capacity of items	**MSS1/E2.1** Make amounts of money up to £1 in different ways using 1p, 2p, 5p, 10p, 20p and 50p coins **MSS1/E2.2** Calculate the cost of more than one item and the change from a transaction, in pence or in whole pounds **MSS1/E2.3** Read and record time in common date formats **MSS1/E2.4** Read and understand time displayed on analogue and 12-hour digital clocks in hours, half hours and quarter hours **MSS1/E2.5** Read, estimate, measure and compare length using common standard and non-standard units (e.g. metre, centimetre, paces) **MSS1/E2.6** Read, estimate, measure and compare weight using common standard units (e.g. kilogram) **MSS1/E2.7** Read, estimate, measure and compare capacity using common standard and non-standard units (e.g. litre, cupful) **MSS1/E2.8** Read and compare positive temperatures in everyday situations such as weather charts **MSS1/E2.9** Read simple scales to the nearest labelled division
Shape and space	**MSS2/E1.1** Recognise and name common 2-D and 3-D shapes **MSS2/E1.2** Understand everyday positional vocabulary (e.g. between, inside or near to)	**MSS2/E2.1** Recognise and name 2-D and 3-D shapes **MSS2/E2.2** Describe the properties of common 2-D and 3-D shapes **MSS2/E2.3** Use positional vocabulary

ENTRY LEVEL 3	LEVEL 1	LEVEL 2
MSS1/E3.1 Add and subtract sums of money using decimal notation **MSS1/E3.2** Round sums of money to the nearest £ and 10p and make approximate calculations **MSS1/E3.3** Read, measure and record time **MSS1/E3.4** Read and interpret distance in everyday situations **MSS1/E3.5** Read, estimate, measure and compare length using non-standard and standard units **MSS1/E3.6** Read, estimate, measure and compare weight using non-standard and standard units **MSS1/E3.7** Read, estimate, measure and compare capacity using non-standard and standard units **MSS1/E3.8** Choose and use appropriate units and measuring instruments **MSS1/E3.9** Read, measure and compare temperature using common units and instruments	**MSS1/L1.1** Add, subtract, multiply and divide sums of money and record **MSS1/L1.2** Read, measure and record time in common date formats and in the 12-hour and 24-hour clock **MSS1/L1.3** Calculate using time **MSS1/L1.4** Read, estimate, measure and compare length, weight, capacity and temperature using common units and instruments **MSS1/L1.5** Read, estimate, measure and compare distance **MSS1/L1.6** Add and subtract common units of measure within the same system **MSS1/L1.7** Convert units of measure in the same system **MSS1/L1.8** Work out the perimeter of simple shapes **MSS1/L1.9** Work out the area of rectangles **MSS1/L1.10** Work out simple volume (e.g. cuboids)	**MSS1/L2.1** Calculate with sums of money and convert between currencies **MSS1/L2.2** Calculate, measure and record time in different formats **MSS1/L2.3** Estimate, measure and compare length, distance, weight and capacity using metric and, where appropriate, imperial units **MSS1/L2.4** Estimate, measure and compare temperature, including reading scales and conversion tables **MSS1/L2.5** Calculate with units of measure within the same system **MSS1/L2.6** Calculate with units of measure between systems, using conversion tables and scales, and approximate conversion factors **MSS1/L2.7** Understand and use given formulae for finding perimeters and areas of regular shapes (e.g. rectangular and circular surfaces) **MSS1/L2.8** Understand and use given formulae for finding areas of composite shapes (e.g. non-rectangular rooms or plots of land) **MSS1/L2.9** Understand and use given formulae for finding volumes of regular shapes (e.g. a cuboid or cylinder) **MSS1/L2.10** Work out dimensions from scale drawings (e.g. 1:20)
MSS2/E3.1 Sort 2-D and 3-D shapes to solve practical problems using properties (e.g. lines of symmetry, side length, angles)	**MSS2/L1.1** Solve problems using the mathematical properties of regular 2-D shapes (e.g. tessellation or symmetry) **MSS2/L1.2** Draw 2-D shapes in different orientations using grids (e.g. in diagrams or plans)	**MSS2/L2.1** Recognise and use common 2-D representations of 3-D objects (e.g. in maps and plans) **MSS2/L2.2** Solve problems involving 2-D shapes and parallel lines (e.g. in laying down carpet tiles)

Handling data: the progression between curriculum elements

	Entry Level	
	ENTRY 1 LEVEL	**ENTRY 2 LEVEL**
Data and statistical measures	**HD1/E1.1** Extract simple information from lists **HD1/E1.2** Sort and classify objects using a single criterion **HD1/E1.3** Construct simple representations or diagrams, using knowledge of numbers, measures or shape and space	**HD1/E2.1** Extract information from lists, tables, simple diagrams and block graphs **HD1/E2.2** Make numerical comparisons from block graphs **HD1/E2.3** Sort and classify objects using two criteria **HD1/E2.4** Collect simple numerical information **HD1/E2.5** Represent information so that it makes sense to others (e.g. in lists, tables and diagrams)
Probability		

ENTRY LEVEL 3	LEVEL 1	LEVEL 2
HD1/E3.1 Extract numerical information from lists, tables, diagrams and simple charts **HD1/E3.2** Make numerical comparisons from bar charts and pictograms **HD1/E3.3** Make observations and record numerical information using a tally **HD1/E3.4** Organise and represent information in different ways so that it makes sense to others	**HD1/L1.1** Extract and interpret information (e.g. in tables, diagrams, charts and line graphs) **HD1/L1.2** Collect, organise and represent discrete data (e.g. in tables, charts, diagrams and line graphs) **HD1/L1.3** Find the arithmetical average (mean) for a set of data **HD1/L1.4** Find the range for a set of data	**HD1/L2.1** Extract discrete and continuous data from tables, diagrams, charts and line graphs **HD1/L2.2** Collect, organise and represent discrete and continuous data in tables, charts, diagrams and line graphs **HD1/L2.3** Find the mean, median and mode, and use them as appropriate to compare two sets of data **HD1/L2.4** Find the range and use it to describe the spread within sets of data
	HD2/L1.1 Show that some events are more likely to occur than others **HD2/L1.2** Express the likelihood of an event using fractions, decimals and percentages with the probability scale of 0 to 1	**HD2/L2.1** Identify the range of possible outcomes of combined events and record the information using diagrams or tables

9. Information and contacts

For information about basic skills, the Basic Skills National Standards, the Adult Literacy Core Curriculum and the Adult Numeracy Core Curriculum contact:

The Basic Skills Agency
Commonwealth House,
1-19 New Oxford Street, London WC1A 1NU
Tel: 020 7405 4017
Fax: 020 7440 6626
Website: **www.basic-skills.co.uk**

For information about the national strategy contact:

Adult Literacy and Numeracy Strategy Unit
Department for Education and Skills
Caxton House – Level 1G
Tothill Street
London SW1H 9NF
andrew.graham@dfee.gov.uk
Website: **www.dfee.gov.uk/readwriteplus**

For leaflets, research documents and publications related to basic skills, contact:

Basic Skills Agency Orderline
Admail 524, London WC1A 1BR
Tel: 0870 600 2400 Fax: 0870 600 2401

For information about signposting to National Training Organisations, contact:

NTO National Council
10 Meadowcourt, Amos Road, Sheffield S9 1BX
Tel: 0114 261 9926
Email: **London@nto-nc.org**

Useful publications include:

Adult Literacy Core Curriculum, The Basic Skills Agency, 2001

Adult Numeracy Core Curriculum, The Basic Skills Agency, 2001

Basic Skills are Union Business, The Basic Skills Agency, 2000

Public Sector, Public Potential, The Basic Skills Agency, 2000

Improving literacy and numeracy – A fresh start, The Basic Skills Agency, 1999